DULL DISASTERS?

DANIEL J. CLARKE

STEFAN DERCON

DULL DISASTERS?

How Planning Ahead Will
Make a Difference

OXFORD
UNIVERSITY PRESS

OXFORD
UNIVERSITY PRESS

Great Clarendon Street, Oxford, OX2 6DP,
United Kingdom

Oxford University Press is a department of the University of Oxford.
It furthers the University's objective of excellence in research, scholarship,
and education by publishing worldwide. Oxford is a registered trade mark of
Oxford University Press in the UK and in certain other countries

Published in the United States of America by Oxford University Press
198 Madison Avenue, New York, NY 10016, United States of America

British Library Cataloguing in Publication Data
Data available

Library of Congress Control Number: 2016933070

ISBN 978–0–19–878557–6

Printed in Great Britain by
Clays Ltd, St Ives plc

Links to third party websites are provided by Oxford in good faith and
for information only. Oxford disclaims any responsibility for the materials
contained in any third party website referenced in this work.

For Pramila, Quentin, Katie, and Emily

PREFACE

This book stems from our urge to communicate that there is a better way of protecting people from the dire effects of natural disasters, particularly in developing countries. As academics and professionals, we have worked on risk and insurance for much of our careers. In the pages that follow, we want to share what we have learned, and, in doing so, contribute to better thought and action on how to shield people and property from the consequences of extreme natural events such as floods, droughts, earthquakes, and pandemics. In short, we will look at how to 'dull' disasters, making sure that such events do not lead to enduring levels of hardship.

One of us, Stefan, has studied for decades how risk affects people in some of the poorest settings in the world, such as in Ethiopia and Tanzania, but also how the poor have devised ingenious ways to limit the consequences of shocks to their incomes and livelihoods. And yet, despite their valiant attempts, they continue to struggle to handle extreme events such as droughts or floods, which have bleak short- and long-term consequences for children and adults. They end up losing their meagre possessions, risk dying too young, or become disabled from poor nutrition. One of the reasons for writing this book is to promote better ways of helping people avoid these outcomes.

Daniel was first a trained actuary, before studying to become an economist. He brings the world of finance and insurance to these problems, asking what can finance do (and what it cannot do) to improve risk management? As researchers, we collaborated in thinking through improving systems for financing risks at the household level. Can insurance ever make sense? Are the current pilot initiatives really offering solutions? Can we find ways of designing insurance systems to complement and strengthen the risk-coping mechanisms poor people already use?

In recent years, we both have become strongly immersed in the world of development policy and practice. Daniel joined the Disaster Risk Financing and Insurance Program, a partnership between the World Bank and the Global Facility for Disaster Reduction and Recovery (GFDRR), designed to help governments and their partners improve how they manage disaster risk. He has worked with some forty developing countries towards implementing the sort of solutions described in this book, and he has seen first-hand the commitment of professionals and the importance of them working together towards politically sellable solutions. Unfortunately, quite a few countries are continuing to find the job of disaster risk management challenging. But there are clearly positive lessons to be learned from other countries, and we share some of these in this book.

Stefan is Chief Economist at the Department for International Development (DFID), the government department responsible for the UK's development aid and policy. At DFID, he advises on more or less anything and everything. Anyone working at DFID, one of the world's largest humanitarian and development donors, cannot help but be struck by the state of the global humanitarian system. It is under pressure—even broke, it is said—drained financially by large and costly conflict-related humanitarian crises. Finding better funding models, at least for problems that are more tractable, such as for natural disasters, is more important than ever.

Both of us are convinced that at both the country and global levels people can be better protected against the dire consequences of extreme natural events. Although what we have learned about risk and insurance is important, we have realized from our work that things poor people themselves have found to work well could serve as models for application nationally and globally. Across the world and throughout history, people have set up what are essentially mutual insurance arrangements in which groups support each other, abiding by clear and credible rules that make the arrangements sustainable. These were the types of arrangements we have studied at the local level in Ethiopia.

Clearly, the national and global challenges in dealing with natural disasters are tougher than the problems these groups can solve. Nevertheless, in this book we will show that the rules and systems these groups use are essentially sound protection principles that could inspire national governments and international agencies as well. It will no doubt not be easy to move towards the new approach laid out in this book. That will require careful technical work as well as courage and commitment by political leaders. Some have risen to this challenge with more credible disaster planning and financing. It is hoped that this book will inspire others to follow.

ACKNOWLEDGEMENTS

A book like this can only grow out of the cumulative efforts of our colleagues working on these questions.

Stefan is particularly grateful to Dessalegn Rahmato for introducing him through his writings to life during drought in Ethiopia before he had ever travelled there. And to Angus Deaton for years ago inspiring him to work on risk and the way people respond to it. Thanks are also due to all his friends, colleagues, and ordinary people he has had the privilege to get to know throughout many years of working in Ethiopia and other poor settings. Without the inspiration they have provided, he would have few thoughts to share. Thanks are also due to his colleagues at the UK Department for International Development (DFID) for the opportunities they have given him, and above all for their integrity and sincerity. To name just some who inspired and supported him to work on this particular topic: Peter D'Souza, Nick Dyer, Nick Harvey, Nick Lea, Mark Lowcock, and Joanna Macrae.

Daniel is particularly grateful to his co-author for his mentorship and intellectual generosity, and to Olivier Mahul for encouraging and helping him to move from theory to practice and for continuing to lead and inspire his team at the World Bank. Thanks also to Samuel Maimbo and Michel Noel, without whom this book would have never been written, and to the long list of others in the World Bank and our client countries who are always generous with their opinions, experience, and stories.

Over the years, and in recent times, we have learned from working with and discussing these topics with Christopher Adam, Orazio Attanasio, Sandra Aviles, Abigail Baca, Dario Bacchini, Charlotte Benson, David Bevan, Tessa Bold, Laura Boudreau, Colin Bruce, Cesar Calvo, Michael Carter, Pin Chantarat, Richard Choularton, Sarah

Coll-Black, Paul Collier, Samantha Cook, Naomi Cooney, Julie Dana, Alain de Janvry, Alejandro del Valle, Carlo del Ninno, Liz Drake, Mareile Drechsler, Chloe Dugger, Marc Forni, Arpine Ghazaryan, Xavier Giné, Francis Ghesquiere, Ric Goodman, Dermot Grenham, Rashmin Gunasekera, Eugene Gurenko, Stephane Hallegatte, Lena Heron, Ruth Vargas Hill, John Hoddinott, Niels Holm-Nielsen, Oscar Ishizawa, Simon James, Pramila Krishnan, Daniel Kull, Josef Lloyd Leitmann, Felix Lung, Barry Maher, Shadreck Mapfumo, Michael Mbaka, Agrotosh Mookerjee, Karlijn Morsink, Andrew Mude, Robert Muir-Wood, Sujoy Mukerji, Rim Nour, Alula Pankhurst, Lydia Poole, Catherine Porter, Richard Poulter, Christoph Pusch, Kolli Rao, Martin Ravallion, Dirk Reinhard, Elisabeth Sadoulet, Alan Sanchez, Rachel Sberro, Reto Schnarwiler, Benedikt Signer, Alanna Simpson, James Sina, Jerry Skees, Emmanuel Skoufias, Wolter Soer, Andrea Stoppa, Charles Stutley, Alemayehu Seyoum Taffesse, Jeremy Tobacman, Niraj Verma, Jose Angel Villalobos, Joachim De Weerdt, Emily White, Tassew Woldehanna, Liam Wren-Lewis, Chris Yiu, and Simon Young. No doubt we forgot to name some.

We would also like to thank our fantastic editor, Sabra Ledent, for her meticulous professional editing. Without her our urge to communicate would not have been fulfilled. Finally, thanks to DFID's Humanitarian Innovation and Evidence Programme and to the Global Facility for Disaster Reduction and Recovery for financial support to write this book.

Everything we have written is the product of our own thoughts, and the usual disclaimers apply. The findings, interpretations, and conclusions expressed, right or wrong, are entirely our own. They do not necessarily represent the views of the UK Department for International Development, those of the International Bank for Reconstruction and Development/World Bank and its affiliated organizations, or those of the executive directors of the World Bank or the governments they represent.

DANIEL J. CLARKE
STEFAN DERCON

CONTENTS

CONTENTS

1

DEALING WITH DISASTERS

It should and can get better

In recent years, typhoons have struck the Philippines and Vanuatu; earthquakes have rocked Haiti, Nepal, Afghanistan, and Pakistan; floods have swept through Pakistan and Mozambique; and droughts have hit Kenya and Somalia. All led to loss of life and livelihoods and destroyed infrastructure, buildings, and businesses.[1] Recovery will take years.

Typhoon Haiyan (Yolanda), which hit the Philippines in November 2013, killed over 7,300 people; the economic losses totalled about US$12.5 billion. In Nepal, more than 8,000 people were killed in the April 2015 earthquake, and many more were injured. Thousands of homes and even entire villages were destroyed, and lives will have to be rebuilt. The 2004 earthquake and tsunami in the Indian Ocean region and the 2010 earthquake in Haiti are still the worst disasters in recent times, each killing more than 200,000 people.

In Kenya, drought affected more than a million farmers in 2014, battering their incomes and their ability to feed their families and keep their children in school. It can be worse: in 2011 drought in the Horn of Africa contributed to tens of thousands of deaths in Somalia, perhaps half of them young children.[2] And it may get even worse: one of the likely effects of climate change is to increase the frequency of the extreme weather events that cause many of these disasters.[3]

Then there was the Ebola virus outbreak in 2014, revealing how a pandemic in very poor countries can wreak havoc. More than 11,000 people were confirmed to have died in Guinea, Liberia, and Sierra Leone.[4]

It would be wrong to suggest the world turns a blind eye when disasters strike. To the contrary, the media usually beam within the country and across the world horrifying images of the suffering. National politicians promise decisive action. Politicians from rich countries voice their concern and publicly instruct agencies to provide crisis funds to offer relief. Global entertainment stars and television news anchors take heavily promoted emotional trips to disaster zones. Ordinary people respond to appeals with generous donations. Volunteers and experts supported by specialized non-governmental organizations (NGOs) and international and government agencies work with the utmost commitment to bring affected areas back to their feet. And across the world, people support the fundamental motivation behind humanitarian aid: that saving lives and alleviating suffering are the right thing to do. Despite this, the disaster responses often seem insufficient, slow, and not well coordinated.

But does it have to be like this? Do extreme events have to turn into disasters with huge losses of life and suffering? Should responses be full of public emotion, painful media images, and political blame games among international, national, and local politicians that nevertheless prove to be slow and inadequate?

We don't think so. But it depends on all those involved declaring their willingness to learn properly from experiences around the world and to apply insights from the latest research across a range of disciplines. In this book, we will show how harnessing the lessons from finance and economics, complemented with evidence from political science, psychology, and the natural sciences, can and does make governments, civil society, private firms, humanitarians, and international organizations much better prepared to deal with natural disasters,[5] thereby reducing the risks to people and economies. We want to make the responses to these events less emotional, less political, less headline-grabbing, and more something that could become 'business as usual'.

What Does This Book Do?

This book lays out the key problems that can cause extreme natural events to turn into natural disasters; takes the reader through a range of solutions that have been implemented around the world to address these problems; provides an overview of what works and what does not based on the evidence; and presents a framework that ties all of this together. Some of these pieces have been analysed individually before, but this book aims to offer a fresh perspective, drawing various strands together for the first time, including the crucial issue of how disasters are financed, which is often overlooked.

We want to persuade our readers that extreme events do not need to lead to as much hardship and loss of life as at present. We are not just making it up: our arguments are based on the latest research and evaluations of past disaster responses worldwide and other academic research. Each chapter also offers, at the end, both a useful recap and a snapshot of the relevant academic literature. These snapshots of the literature convey the research foundation of our narrative and are a guide to a more in-depth treatment.

What this book does not do is criticize the thousands of deeply committed individuals working tirelessly to bring relief to disaster-torn areas and to prevent further suffering. Our critique is about the national and international systems behind these people, and how there is still a widespread systemic failure to prepare for disaster before it strikes. Our main thesis, which is developed, motivated, and inter-rogated throughout the book, is that three things need to be put in place before a disaster to protect lives and livelihoods:

1. A coordinated plan for post-disaster action agreed in advance
2. A fast, evidence-based decision-making process
3. Financing on standby to ensure that the plan can be implemented.

If these three things seem obvious, there are plenty of examples in which some or all of them were not in place, resulting in unnecessary suffering and economic losses. More important, they are not systematically embedded in national and global disaster response systems.

A myriad of agencies at the national and international levels are entrusted with providing short-term support to those in need when a disaster strikes in order to save lives and alleviate suffering. They are the agencies and departments of local and national governments, various agencies of the United Nations, and national and international NGOs. Collectively, these agencies and their funders are known as the *global humanitarian system*.[6] There is also a range of institutions that support the more medium- and long-term responses and reconstruction after disasters, including national governments, donor governments, and development financial institutions such as the World Bank and regional development banks.

We believe this system has serious flaws. The post-disaster decision-making process is far too politicized, leading to delays, poor decisions, and bad coordination of effort. Recent disasters such as the earthquake in Nepal or Ebola in West Africa are good case studies of the commitments nationally and internationally to provide support, but also of what can go wrong in decision making and the consequences. The good news is that insights from economists and political and behavioural scientists are at hand to improve this situation. And science is helping to achieve much better predictions of when disasters will occur and the damage they will cause. But those affected need more than early warning; they need early action that is evidence-based and fast.

Fast decisions are only sensible if they are related to credible, coordinated plans. Every time a natural disaster hits any part of the world, the newspaper headlines ten days later can be written in advance: 'Why isn't the response more coordinated? Still no food or water for some areas'. The truth is, everybody argues for coordination but nobody likes to be coordinated.

Evaluations of recent disaster responses contain vivid examples of these coordination failures. For example, a cross-agency report on the earthquake response in 2010 in Haiti found that there was very poor coordination among humanitarian aid organizations after the earth-quake; their responses lacked planning and thus were poorly adapted to local circumstances. Many parallel structures were set up inside and outside government, duplicating effort and feeding coordination failures and power battles.[7] Evaluations of the response to Typhoon Haiyan in the Philippines in 2013 highlighted similar failures.[8] A large response followed, but international donors were unaware of national structures and capacity. Differences in understanding between the international humanitarian community and the local government of emergency relief and recovery phases led to poor coordination and parallel structures.[9]

Poor coordination and an ineffective response are not only the standard findings in developing countries. In 2005 Hurricane Katrina slammed into New Orleans in the US state of Louisiana. The storm and the subsequent floods killed more than 1,200 people and caused possibly US$100 billion in losses. Official evaluations found that the losses caused by the hurricane stemmed in part from questionable leadership decisions and capabilities, organizational failures, over-whelmed rescue and communication systems, and poor multi-agency coordination leading to a duplication of effort.[10] What seems com-mon sense is rarely in place: a careful, pre-financed plan that has been approved by all who might be called on to offer support.

Our strongest criticism of the current disaster responses relates to the way they are financed (post-disaster with no careful pre-disaster planning). Fortunately, insights from economics and finance can help solve this problem. At the moment, much of the response to disasters as well as the entire humanitarian system are funded by voluntary contributions, collected via appeals to donor governments and the public after a disaster takes place. National and local governments also scramble for resources by reallocating from other budgets. It is as if financial instruments such as insurance do not exist.

Meanwhile, appeals are not far off from begging bowls, and govern-ments and donors seem at times to resemble benefactors for a good cause and saviours coming to the rescue rather than participants in an organized system in which responses and routes to recovery are carefully planned beforehand using sound financial instruments. Begging bowls and benefactors—this is a system built on medieval financial principles. Although science may not always be able to predict exactly when and where a natural disaster will strike, it can assess the likelihood of different disasters occurring, and disaster-management professionals can assess what response would be useful after each potential disaster. Taken together, these two capabilities mean that financial planning for sensible disaster response and recovery is possible. Despite this, the current systems appear to ignore centuries of progress in developing better financial instruments that can be put to good use to the benefit of those unlucky enough to be affected by disasters.

The Evidence?

One can easily predict the conclusions drawn from evaluations and reviews of any disaster response programme a few years later. This government or agency 'wasn't well enough prepared, and also it should have invested more in disaster risk reduction and resilience of communities'. 'The international aid that was supposed to come in arrived too late.'[11] Such evaluations will also point out that the 'local roads were not rebuilt for years because of a disagreement between the local and national government over who would pay for reconstruction'. The way humanitarian and development support is financed is crucial here: the financing of the system has to ensure that there are strong incentives for credible planning and disaster risk reduction—not just to sit around and wait for a bailout.

Development—that is, a stronger and more inclusive economy and society—is the best form of resilience to a natural disaster.[12] This will take time, and even then natural hazards will not go away, especially with climate change lurking. Both the way the national and global humanitarian system is organized and the way it is financed ignore the fact that the incentives for disaster risk reduction and for making

6

countries and communities far more resilient to natural disasters are rather poor, and at best an afterthought. And even if the lessons highlighted are starkest for the developing world, in rich societies these lessons remain valid. In the United States, failures in decision making and preparedness planning, poor risk reduction, and the faults in the ways in which response and recovery finance were organized also contributed to greater loss of life and more misery from Hurricane Katrina and the subsequent floods than there should have been.[13]

There are also plenty of examples—some of them recent and novel—in which seemingly minor developments in the way disasters are planned for and financed have had significant positive impacts on people's lives. In all examples, the bulk of the planning happens before the disaster and involves pre-disaster commitments over who will do what and who will pay for what. In Kenya, for example, donors, NGOs, the World Bank, and the government are working together in the Hunger Safety Net Programme. Under this programme, pastoralists receive what is effectively an insurance policy—a social safety net that, without delay and questions, pays a cash transfer to a pre-defined group when the rains fail and the harvest is bad so they can afford to buy inputs and food for their families. For even more peace of mind, they also are given the option of buying affordable insurance to keep their animals alive. The scheme has simple triggers; donors and government co-finance it; and costly needs assessments and delays are avoided. It allows pastoralists to invest in their cows, goats, and camels without worry that the next drought will ruin them.[14]

In Mexico, the country's National Disaster Fund, FONDEN (El Fondo Nacional para el Desarrollo Nacional), operates a rules-based system to reconstruct public infrastructure such as roads, hospitals, and schools after a disaster hits. In this collaboration among the federal government, state governments, and the private sector, everyone has agreed to an objective procedure to determine the degree of damage, and the processes are implemented by an independent third party and audited by all parties. The result is clarity pre-disaster over who will pay for what. FONDEN also offers incentives for risk reduction, rewarding such investments. Financial markets are used to lock in this rules-based approach.[15]

In India, the government and farmers share the cost of crop insurance that allows cheaper input credit because the banks can now trust that farmers will be able to repay even if their harvests fail. Meanwhile, farmers are protected and able to invest more in their farms.

In Ethiopia, a major drought in part of the country in 2011 did not result in major loss of life (unlike in Somalia). One important reason was that the government, with donor support, had set up the Productive Safety Net Programme, which was designed to be scaled up to absorb more funding and reach more people during a crisis. In 2011 it managed to expand to support 9.6 million people. This was quite a different result from the 1984–5 drought when more than 400,000—and possibly as many as 1 million—people perished when the country was in the midst of a civil war.[16]

So why aren't there more of these schemes?

These examples from Kenya, Mexico, India, and Ethiopia have strong similarities. In all these countries, governments and plenty of local and international players are willing to provide support if natural hazards cause hardship. Acting on that willingness, all the parties involved have worked to be prepared in a credible way so that after a disaster the government and its partners can make a political announcement that the system is working rather than having to announce a new ad-hoc initiative. The decision-making process for the response is rules-based and transparent. The nature of the response is defined clearly beforehand. And the financing is organized in a credible way.

In fact, these countries have unintentionally organized themselves as if they are part of an insurance system, using similar principles. It is clear which risks are protected and which are not, and who is responsible for covering what, as if governments and their partners entered into a contract with the individuals and communities involved. These countries gained credibility by ensuring that the financing is in place, including using forms of insurance and reinsurance (India, Kenya, and

Mexico). They agreed up front to cost-sharing rules between government and donors (Kenya and Ethiopia), state governments (India and Mexico), and the individuals protected (India and Kenya). And they were all conscious of the incentives for moral hazard that plague insurance markets (whereby insurance may induce those covered to stop reducing risk because they are now covered). Like a good insurance system, then, they have tried to design systems that offer incentives for disaster risk reduction.

What is described here is a far cry from the shocking images, media appeals, fund raising, and moral arm-twisting that normally follow a disaster because underlying these programmes are insurance and other financial products. And they are more about accountants, financial management, planning meetings, data, decision-making rules, and well-prepared logistics. This is our purpose: we want to make disasters business as usual, not hand-wringing as usual.

A Focus on Natural Disasters

This book is not about every form of human hardship: across the world, hundreds of millions people are suffering from hunger and despair, and are even at risk of survival from circumstances beyond their control. We focus here on extreme natural events and their consequences. We consider what are called 'fast-onset' disasters, linked to sudden events such as earthquakes, floods, and storms, which require an immediate response to protect lives as well as a longer-term recovery from the destruction of homes, infrastructure, and livelihoods. We also discuss slow-onset disasters, which may start slowly, but their effects, such as drought and pandemic, become worse over time, threatening lives and livelihoods. No matter the type of disaster, however, a timely response is key: the later the response, the worse the consequences.

Although this book deals with disasters triggered by extreme natural events, we are very aware that there are other demands for a large-scale response based on the humanitarian system and the generosity of people and government that are not covered here. Despite involving billions of dollars each year, spending via international agencies and donors on humanitarian crises related to natural events, including pandemics, is smaller than spending on crises linked to conflict. What has been happening in Syria is a clear example. Massive humanitarian support is needed for the populations affected by conflict, including internally displaced populations and refugee populations outside the country's borders. These conflict-induced crises tend to last many years, leading to protracted suffering. The financial costs of these responses are collectively many billions per year, often with little prospect of resolution and recovery.

Our approach can offer ideas on how to respond to conflict-induced crises better, not least in the early stages, but there are important differences between these crises and those stemming from natural disasters that will make a successful and a more cost-effective response far harder. We do not want to claim that our approach is applicable in any kind of simplistic way. Nevertheless, some of the lessons on response plans, decision making, and financial planning should offer food for thought for conflict-induced crises as well. It is true in any case that if the global humanitarian system were to use the principles advocated in this book to organize its support for the disasters following extreme natural events, it could focus its intellectual and financial resources much better on handling these other crises.

Let's Dull Disasters!

Economic losses from disasters such as earthquakes, tsunamis, cyclones, and flooding are now reaching an average of US$250–$300 billion a year.[17] In the last twenty years, more than 530,000 people died as a direct result of approximately 15,000 extreme weather events alone; millions of people were seriously injured. Most of the deaths and serious injuries were in developing countries.[18]

Meanwhile, highly infectious diseases will continue to emerge or re-emerge. Natural hazards will not disappear—earthquakes, storms, and droughts will continue to pose threats. There will be loss of life and destruction of infrastructure and houses. Lives and livelihoods will be affected for thousands of people. But, as this book will show, these extreme events do not need to turn into large-scale humanitarian disasters. Better and faster responses are possible. Faster recovery with much less hardship or permanent losses of assets and livelihoods is achievable. Learning from the weaknesses of the current responses and their financing is the first step. Our thesis is that even though there is much generosity in the world to support the responses to and recovery from natural disasters, the funding model, based on mobilizing financial resources after disasters take place, is flawed and makes responses ineffective and late. Being generous after a disaster is too late. The way forward is to act before disasters strike, preparing credible plans with rules-based decision-making and early action and held together with sound financial planning agreed beforehand.

This is not just a technical matter. It will involve political courage and commitment by leaders across the world. If successful, it will make a disaster response less of a media spectacle fraught with emotion and adrenaline. Indeed, it may make disasters a little duller for the twenty-four-hour news outlets. But, most important, it will result in disasters that have a less intense impact, as in the other meaning of 'dull'. Dulling disasters is what this book is all about.

Recapping...

1. The world does not turn a blind eye to disasters. Many disasters are followed by an outpouring of generosity.
2. Despite this, disaster responses often seem insufficient, slow, and not well coordinated, and recovery can take years.
3. The main thesis of this book is that the impact of disasters can be dulled if three things are in place beforehand:

- A coordinated plan for post-disaster action agreed in advance
- A fast, evidence-based decision-making process
- Financing on standby to ensure that the plan can be implemented.

4. The solutions we present throughout this book are based on pre-agreed, pre-financed, rules-based plans that can be implemented after a disaster without the need for further political decisions.

2

DEFINING THE PROBLEM

Begging bowls and benefactors

There is something predictable about the way most of us learn about a natural disaster. It usually starts with a news item on the radio or television or a Tweet or news alert on a mobile phone. Fast-onset disasters, such as earthquakes or floods, always tend to make the headlines. Then reports of the estimated numbers of lives lost and of the damage caused begin to come in. Politicians and senior officials may strut before the cameras to demonstrate their leadership by embracing the three C's of crisis management: *concern* about the situation and suffering, *commitment* to do something about it, and *control* of the situation. When disasters take place in relatively poorer countries, appeals for aid are quickly broadcast: they take the form of requests for help from local communities or national governments and formal appeals to richer countries for contributions to inter-national agencies or to the public for contributions to non-governmental organizations (NGOs).

So it was for the Nepal earthquake in April 2015.[1] Within a few days, extensive reports of damage and loss of life were followed by an appeal by the United Nations for US$415 million to cover the first three months of relief efforts. Across the world media, NGOs appealed for donations to their efforts on the ground. For slow-onset disasters such as a drought or a viral outbreak such as Ebola, it is typically not that much different except that the crisis may not reach the news headlines until it becomes visible, and even then substantial airtime and social-media discussions are devoted to debating whether it really is a disaster.

Once a crisis is clearly imminent, expectations of leadership by politicians and international organizations, media attention, and appeals for support are front and centre. What happens next is also predictable: frustration, fallout, and blame games. Support often comes late, and when it finally arrives it is described as ineffectual and insufficient. Those in need expect the authorities to help them, and those delivering the help seem underprepared and underfunded, and they begin to spar publicly. Nepal was no exception. Within days, media reports noted the slow progress of the response, and the political fallout.[2]

All this makes good news copy, but something more profound is also at play. There is a clear expectation from those in need, as well as those seeing need, that assistance will be given. The moral obligation to help people undergoing hardship because of events clearly beyond their control is well accepted; indeed, even the most diehard opponents of international aid sense that humanitarian support is right and reasonable. This global concern is embedded in international declarations, including the global commitments in UN General Assembly Resolution 46/182, 1991, which offers humanitarian principles. The first of these principles, that of 'humanity', states: 'Human suffering must be addressed wherever it is found. The purpose of humanitarian action is to protect life and health and ensure respect for human beings.' There is, of course, nothing wrong with this principle— indeed, quite the contrary.

But how is this principle put into practice? Usually not well. Responses to natural disasters need to be timely and on the right scale. For example, how local and national governments and international agencies respond in the immediate aftermath of earthquakes is crucial to protect lives and livelihoods in the short term, but also to restrict the scale of the long-term consequences. An early response in slow-onset disasters is just as critical. As the spread of the Ebola virus in Africa revealed, containing an Ebola outbreak when there are just a few dozen or a few hundred cases—as was the case in Uganda in 2004 and in the Democratic Republic of Congo in 2014—is far less costly and far easier than when thousands of people are infected—which was the situation by August 2014 in West Africa when the World Health Organization (WHO) declared the epidemic a Public Health Emergency of International Concern and a major international response was launched. According to data from Kenya and Ethiopia, substantially more lives and millions of dollars can be saved by an early response to a drought compared with a later response.[3]

Behind these delays is recurring ambiguity about who is in charge beforehand to plan and finance the consequences of these extreme events—that is, who should be taking on the risk and preparing for a response. This ambiguity leads, in turn, to poor plans and poor financing arrangements, despite many statements by all concerned that all human suffering will receive a response.

A Flawed Funding Model

Working backwards from the way responses are financed sheds light on why this process goes wrong. When a disaster strikes, the first point of call is usually the government, at both the local and national levels. Across the world, governments are usually keen to respond, but they often do not have large contingency budgets—that is, budgets that are spent only if something exceptional occurs. Even if a government had such a budget, it may have already been spent. During a disaster-related crisis, cash needs to be mobilized, but either this requires new borrowing (essentially running an overdraft), or a government must reallocate funding from other budgets. This means it is not free money, and it will have a cost. For example, cash may have to be raised by cutting government services such as maintaining roads. In richer countries, borrowing or reallocating funds would be difficult and costly but politically important enough that it would go forward. For poor countries, its consequences would be worse because spending is typically already tight, borrowing is more costly, and reallocations may affect basic government functions. These countries, then, are likely to turn to global humanitarian agencies and development partners for support.

The parties making up the humanitarian system also do not have large contingency budgets; they operate with something that resembles a cash budget (spending only the resources that are available). As of December 2015, the humanitarian need (the sum of all global UN appeals) stood at US$20 billion, but only about 50 per cent of that amount was funded.[4] Behind this scale of underfunding is a deeply flawed funding model: appeals, linked to a particular crisis. All the main international agencies and NGOs involved are largely funded through appeals that solicit voluntary contributions from governments and the general public. The size of contributions is not pre-specified; in fact, no one is obliged to contribute. In the same way, many poorer countries appeal directly to the international community for support after disasters—an approach that leads to very uneven funding and recurring large funding gaps.

This ad-hoc, post-disaster model for financing disasters is hardly worthy of the twenty-first century. In fact, it feels distinctly medieval. It is a funding model based on begging bowls, whereby individuals, communities, local and national governments, international agencies, and NGOs are required to play the part of a beggar, as though they are pleading for alms, sitting in a row in front of a medieval cathedral or mosque. Benefactors may well be committed to digging in their pockets to share their coins with those who clearly are facing hardship, but their coins may run out midway through the row. Without more information, the benefactors do not know which beggars are the neediest, and so the neediest might not receive the most benefits. In short, begging has hardly ever been a stable source of resources to deal with the vagaries of life, not least when time is of the essence and benefactors need to make very quick decisions based on limited information.

The Consequences

The consequences of a financial model that encourages reasonable people and organizations to play the part of a beggar after each disaster can be dire.

Ambiguities

The model creates ambiguity about who owns the risk: who will need to act and who will need to pay for it. Across the world, national and local governments and politicians will say with confidence that in the first instance they do. As for developing countries, the various agencies of the United Nations, such as the United Nations High Commissioner for Refugees (UNHCR), World Food Programme (WFP), World Health Organization (WHO), United Nations Children's Fund (UNICEF), and United Nations Office of the Coordinator of Humanitarian Affairs (OCHA), as well as various big donors, will all claim they are there to work with governments so that the appropriate responses and financing materialize. Local and international NGOs and the International Federation of Red Cross and Red Crescent Societies (IFRC) will also claim to be responsible for responding to crises.

All this is reasonable, and in fact governments should have key responsibilities. But across all organizations, such statements are hollow because there is no guaranteed financing for fulfilling promises. Credibility requires a finance model that will deliver the funds when needed. Within countries, the lack of clarity between national and local governments over who should respond and who should finance the response leads to ineffectual relief efforts. Evaluations of the response to Hurricane Katrina in 2005 in the United States brought this home.[5]

The Ebola outbreak in West Africa in 2014 was another example of a situation in which a lack of clarity on who owned the risk and response was at the core of long delays. Most observers expected the national governments to own the risk, with WHO offering a second layer of risk protection in terms of expertise and finance if governments could not handle it. Indeed, this is how previous outbreaks of Ebola had been managed. This time, however, national governments were unable to contain the epidemic, and WHO did not have the resources to act at scale on this widespread expectation. Large bilateral donors and their agencies were not *prepared* to respond quickly once this became clear because they did not realize they were carrying the risk, and therefore they did not have the plans and preparation in place to scale up to deliver on the response quickly. The result: valuable time was lost, and, as evaluation reports have shown, the long period of inaction led to more misery and higher costs.[6] One study suggested that a response one month earlier could have averted more than half the cases in Sierra Leone.[7]

Procrastination and Delays

The lack of pre-commitment embedded in begging-bowl financing also leads to one of the enemies of effective decision making: procrastination among implementers as well as donors. Procrastination, the decision to delay or postpone something, is a well-studied phenomenon affecting the decision making of individuals or groups. According to the research, when they are faced with a decision on whether to act but the choice is not obvious, or when the action required is demanding and difficult, inaction is the common response.[8] In many recent cases, including slow-onset disasters such as droughts and pandemics, this has been a real problem. Responding to a possible large-scale disaster early is harder than taking no action at all, especially because funding needs to be found at the right scale. The result is a tendency to procrastinate over acting and committing funding. This phenomenon was present in the national and international decision making around the Ebola response in West Africa, as well as in the responses to the 2010–11 drought in Somalia and the neighbouring regions[9] and in the recent responses to likely extreme weather events linked to El Niño. Crises tend to be rather well developed before decisions are made to respond.

Crying Wolf

Actually, the consequences of begging-bowl financing can be worse. A funding model based on voluntary contributions and appeals does not just risk underfunding some causes, thereby leading to delays and more suffering. It also creates serious distortions and bad incentives that make poor responses more likely. Because underfunding is common and little pre-committed funding is available, strong incentives surface among the implementing agencies to exaggerate crises and appeals. In June 2011, a UN press release suggested and was interpreted by the international media as meaning that in East Africa the worst drought in sixty years was under way.[10] The truth, however, was that it was the worst drought in a relatively small number of specific pastoralist areas in Somalia, Kenya, and Ethiopia. No doubt, a bad drought was taking place, but the press release was somewhat parsimonious with the truth. Raising false alarms, 'crying wolf' as in Aesop's famous fable, is a big risk here: because potential donors are aware of the incentives for overstatement, many appeals will hardly receive a response. As it turned out, this particular crisis did end up in a massive human disaster because the drought coincided with the raging conflict in Somalia, and responses were late and ineffective.[11] It was not evident, however, that more finance would have avoided the crisis.

Such an exaggeration for effect is not uncommon, and rarely does one hear of retractions when the media overstate risks. For example, some agencies' declarations and media reports that West Africa was at risk of famine during the Ebola outbreak in 2014 did not quite have a truthful ring to them based on the evidence available. If the information to be used for decision making is manipulated to overstate the need, it is difficult for those contributing to the system to make sensible trade-offs over where and when to contribute.

Fragmented Responses

The funding model also needs political or other leaders to be *seen* as doing the right thing. And when the cameras are rolling and after the crisis has already unfolded, this is the right time to fill the begging bowl and offer its proceeds to those in need. But for many disasters, this is too late. That said, let us be clear: there is nothing wrong with this media attention, and there is nothing wrong with opportunities for politicians and other leaders to show leadership. Indeed, there is much research to suggest that political leadership ensures that natural hazards do not turn into disasters, and its absence can cause serious failures—such as in the case of Hurricane Katrina in 2005, in Haiti in 2010, and in the late responses to the Ebola virus in West Africa in 2014. An active press is also an effective mechanism for accountability and better responses. Nobel laureate Amartya Sen argued long ago that media attention ensured the disappearance of famines in India after independence.[12] Subsequent research revealed how the press and better competitive elections made this true for the quality of response across India.[13]

Meanwhile, another consequence of lack of pre-commitment of financing to plans and implementers is the incentives it creates for flag planting and limelight hugging. 'Everyone loves a good drought', as the Indian journalist Palagummi Sainath famously wrote.[14] A humanitarian crisis allows the flags of nations and organizations to be planted, showcasing their generosity and success. Internationally and locally, a crisis allows politicians to show leadership and seek to portray themselves as the saviours of those experiencing hardship. Everyone wants to hug the limelight and show off their effectiveness. But that kind of grandstanding only exacerbates the incentives for fragmentation rather than coordination: going it alone makes it easier to claim to be at the centre of the response, whether as a funder or an implementer. And it creates a class of benefactors: leaders in receiving and donor countries and in local and international organizations who can choose which begging bowl to fill or what to do with their available cash. Planning beforehand would have seemed futile since financing only follows a disaster. Therefore, these benefactors will play a direct role in deciding what the response will look like and how the subsequent recovery will roll out.

With this funding model, no organization can guarantee before the onset of disasters that it can offer the right response. Because funding is not secure, the overall picture is one of incentives for extensive fragmentation when crises occur rather than for coordination. Each organization may have plans, but without guaranteed funding of their plans none can act. The result is a dispersed, unwieldy system with much multiplication rather than economies of scale. Those who can mobilize resources respond, and so whenever a disaster develops, dozens of national aid agencies, international organizations, and NGOs all get involved. But each must be sustained, and each needs resources. Local governments, national leaders, international donors, and multilateral agencies also vie for their roles: all claim to recognize the importance of coordination, and yet none of them wants to be coordinated.

Disaster Risk Reduction and Preparedness

A funding model based on appeals and other begging bowls hardly encourages national or international organizations to undertake serious investments in reducing the risk of a disaster and preparedness. After all, if an organization has no idea how much funding might be available, how can it plan for the appropriate scale of response? Without a secure budget, how can it invest before a disaster in a post-disaster implementation capacity?

But it gets worse. Benefactors are anointed in full view, not from quiet graft in the shadows. A politician probably will not get *credit* for pushing good preparedness plans and investments. Plus, such planning demands more effort for limited immediate gain. Only lip service will be paid to investments in early warning systems, preventive infrastructure investments, building codes and zoning, and education and technical assistance in preparedness. Why should a politician invest in a sensible system to reduce risks and enable a quick response to a strong earthquake if the political benefits from such a system are likely to be reaped by that politician's political successor? These facts of political life tend to lead to procrastination in setting up good response systems beforehand and in delays in making firm decisions about how to respond under various circumstances—after all, decision makers are under little pressure and the rewards are scarce. And risk-reduction investments will lose out.

There is good evidence that electoral politics tends to encourage these behaviours: political leaders are rewarded by the voters for offering disaster relief, while disaster preparedness has no impact on election outcomes. For example, in India incumbent parties are apparently rewarded if they vigorously respond to disastrous weather events, but only in election years. Relief is much higher, then, in such years.[15] These electoral behaviours are also observed in the United States. Presidential disaster declarations in affected states are rewarded by the electorate, but a president is punished if a governor's request for relief is denied.[16] These behaviours skew incentives in the choice between relief and preparedness: voters reward the delivery of disaster relief, but not investments in disaster preparedness.[17] Improving disaster responses and preparedness will require balancing these incentives.

Moving Beyond a Medieval System of Finance

So, how can countries and their partners do better in handling disasters? They surely can go beyond a medieval system of finance that ignores centuries of progress in developing insurance and other financial protection instruments. Modern financial principles can ensure certainty in finance in a world of uncertainty.

But decision makers do not necessarily have to go to the City of London or to Wall Street for ideas and advice. Across the world, communities have long experimented with finding ways of protecting themselves against disasters. For example, slum dwellers in Dhaka, the capital of Bangladesh, can teach them a few things. The buildings in the slums are built of woven bamboo, and food is cooked inside over open fires. Highly combustible, the dwellings often catch fire, destroying dozens of homes and shops in one go. There is no fire insurance for such informally planned settlements or public compensation after fires. The solution? Residents have set up groups of a few dozen or more members. Each week, a cashier collects a fixed amount of money from each member and banks it. In the event of a fire, the money is withdrawn and distributed to the members in proportion to their contribution. This is an extremely simple form of a reserve or contingency fund, pooled to ensure that it is only used for the designated purpose: paying for fire losses. When a fire occurs, the cash for compensation is readily available and disbursed using clear and simple rules.[18]

Poor people's funeral insurance systems across the world also offer up some lessons. Among the fisherfolk in Cochin in Kerala, India, early death is all too common. However, funerals can be very expensive, and cash is not readily available when someone dies. Members of the annual burial fund pay in a fixed sum each week for a year. If the member or a close relative dies, a payout is offered from the fund, no strings attached. At the end of the year, if any funds remain they are distributed to the members. If the fund runs out of cash during the year, all members are asked to make up the shortfalls in equal shares.[19]

The funeral group operated by Muungano, the village union of women's groups in the small village of Nyakatoke in Western Tanzania, provides insurance that supplements what the traditional village Bujuni (or 'mutual help') association offers at the time of mourning. The additional protection involves only a small contribution beforehand, but when someone dies a strictly enforced commitment goes into effect, and a particular sum of cash is paid by each member to the deceased family, plus a fixed contribution in kind or in labour.[20] In recent years, these groups have expanded their coverage and now also offer a payout when someone needs to be hospitalized.

Ethiopia has its own version of these funeral societies, usually called *iddirs* (see Chapter 4). They are based on a simple model, similar to the one found in Cochin.

All these schemes are group-based versions of insurance, with fixed regular contributions and fixed payouts when a fire, death, or serious illness occurs. Such groups are at the root of many of the largest insurance companies in the world. They operate as a mutual fund, a 'risk pool' of savings, which is used to pay for pre-specified risks.[21]

These examples from around the world point to the kind of finance model for disaster responses and recovery that would overcome many of the disincentives and failures of the current system of voluntary contributions after disasters have unfolded. It uses insurance principles to finance need and states clearly exactly who holds the risk: for example, the funeral society's fund based on members' contributions pays for the costs of funerals and possibly other pre-specified risks. Contributions are collected beforehand and predictable—no begging bowls required, or at least liabilities are well defined. The ways in which to raise extra emergency cash are specified. There is no ambiguity, no gaming, no procrastination.

These, then, are the elements of a sensible model to deal with the response to calamities internationally and within countries. The system is based on clear-cut decision rules, and there is no ambiguity about who owns the risk, who needs to respond, and how it is financed. The incentives to prepare a response and to reduce risks are in place. And, finally, a financing model offers resources when they are needed, turning risk and uncertainty into the certainty of support. No more begging bowls or benefactors.

This is a big ask for political leaders for whom discretion is the default setting. But in the chapters that follow, we outline how this can be done. Planners will begin by putting together and packaging politically sellable alternatives to begging-bowl financing, including thinking through who will be protected and against what, who will pay, and what the conditions for protection will be (Chapter 3). Then, in moving from discretion to rules, they will think carefully about what data will trigger action, and how it will be collected and protected from fraud and political opportunism (Chapter 4). Finally, planners will help benefactors to pre-commit their funds before disasters strike in ways that encourage coordination and proper incentives for risk reduction (Chapter 5).

Recapping...

1. The post-disaster relationships between national and subnational governments, governments and farmers, governments and homeowners, and governments and the international humanitarian system often take the form of a begging bowl, although there are notable exceptions.
2. Begging bowls arise because of benefactors—the people who retain discretion over how to allocate their budgets after a disaster strikes.
3. For beneficiaries, begging-bowl financing of disaster risk is fraught with uncertainty—they do not know what help to expect and when help will arrive. It can also undermine their incentives to invest in disaster risk reduction and preparedness. All of these factors can increase the economic and human costs of catastrophes.

A Snapshot of the Literature

The effect of an altruistic benefactor on the risk-reduction investments made by a vulnerable beneficiary has been considered in depth in economic research. Situations in which the benefactor can provide post-disaster relief but cannot condition that relief on the pre-disaster behaviour of the beneficiary are a special case of a much more general situation known as *hidden action*, or *moral hazard* (Arrow 1971; Hölmstrom 1979). In the context of disaster risk, the beneficiary has fewer incentives to invest in *self-protection*, such as strengthening buildings against natural hazards such as earthquakes, limiting development to low-risk areas, shifting to economic activities that are more resilient, or purchasing insurance themselves (Kaplow 1991). This finding is sometimes referred to as a type of *Samaritan's Dilemma* (Buchanan 1975; Lindbeck and Weibull 1988; Coate 1995) or more recently as a *Charity Hazard* (Browne and Hoyt 2000; Raschky and

Weck-Hannemann 2007). Cohen and Werker (2008) offer a political-economy version, applying it to case studies of disaster relief.

A large empirical literature confirms this prediction more rigorously for both the general case and national disaster-relief programs. For example, Kousky et al. (2013) consider floods in the United States and estimate that for every US$1 increase in average relief investment, self-protection in the form of insurance decreases by approximately US$6. Van Asseldonk et al. (2002) found that Dutch farmers who believed government assistance would be available in the event of a disaster had a significantly lower demand for crop insurance.

Meanwhile, political scientists have offered a variety of explanations for underspending on disaster preparedness and overspending on disaster relief by national governments. First, voters may show a *preference for private goods*, such as direct relief payments, over public goods, such as investments in early warning systems or better building codes and zoning. Second, voters may simply be *less aware of the benefits of disaster preparedness expenditures relative to disaster relief expenditures* because of their lower relevance to them and the reduced media coverage. Third, voters may make *attribution errors* by attributing investments in preparedness expenditures to future government administrations, whereas they are more likely to attribute relief expenditures to the current administration. This attribution error reduces politicians' incentives to make long-term investments in risk reduction. Fourth, voters may find it difficult to quantify the benefits from investments in risk reduction, and in particular to construct *counterfactuals* for how much larger the loss would have been after a disaster without risk-reduction investments. Without such a comparison, they may underappreciate disaster preparedness expenditures. Finally, voters may be *shortsighted* and underappreciate long-term investments in risk reduction that do not yield large short-term pay-offs. Healy and Malhotra (2009) analysed these five potential mechanisms using a data set on natural disasters, U.S. government spending, and election returns, and found that the first mechanism, the desire for individually targeted goods over public goods, went a long way towards providing a useful explanation for the behaviour of US politicians. They also estimated that federal investments in preparedness are extremely cost-effective, with every US$1 spent on preparedness leading to a reduction in damage of approximately $15.

Beyond Healy and Malhotra (2009), there is a wide range of evidence that disaster relief buys votes. For example, using data on rainfall, public relief spending, and elections from India, Cole et al. (2012) found that voters punish the incumbent party for weather events beyond its control, but they punish the incumbent party less when it vigorously responds to an event. This effect, however, is limited to election years. Correspondingly, the authors find that the government spends more on relief in election years. Reeves (2011) demonstrates that in the United States between 1981 and 2004 a single presidential disaster declaration to specific constituencies translated on average into a one-point increase in votes for the presidential party in a state-wide contest. Furthermore, when the president rejects a governor's request for federal assistance, the president is punished in voting, whereas the governor is rewarded (Gasper and Reeves 2011). Fuchs and Rodriguez-Chamussy (2014) analysed the impact of insurance payouts on voter behaviour in the 2006 Mexican presidential election. In this study, the incumbent party was estimated to have garnered 8 per cent more votes where payments were made prior to the election. Eisensee and Strömberg (2007) explain US disaster relief payments by media coverage, showing that when a disaster occurs simultaneously with other newsworthy events such as the Olympic Games, post-disaster aid is reduced because media coverage of the disaster is crowded out by the other events.

Although there are probably a large variety of reasons behind delays in the provision of disaster relief, one reason may be the strategic behaviour of benefactors. It is well understood that strategic situations in which multiple parties could voluntarily contribute to achieving a common goal—in this case the provision of relief to disaster victims by multiple potential benefactors—often lead to the observance of strategic delays (Osborne and Rubinstein 1990). Some convincing evidence of the cost of such delays has been uncovered. For example, looking at extreme droughts, Alderman et al. (2003) investigated the impact of preschool malnutrition on subsequent human-capital formation in rural Zimbabwe. The authors estimated that reduced nutrition in children under 2 may lead to a loss of 14 per cent of lifetime earnings. Using Ethiopian data, Dercon (2004) estimated the effects of rainfall on consumption growth. He found that, as a result of reduced consumption and increased distress sales, household income at the end of the nine-year study period was 16 per cent lower than that of households that had not suffered to the same degree. Clarke and Hill (2013) used these two studies to estimate that responding early in an extreme slow-onset drought would have been approximately three times more cost-effective than responding late.

3

BRING IN THE PROFESSIONALS

Homer, the great Greek poet, wrote several millennia ago about Odysseus and his adventures. One of the most famous passages of the *Odyssey* illustrates the virtue of a sensible plan and the need to commit beforehand when difficult times are ahead. In this passage, his hero's sea travels take him and his ship's crew close to the Sirenusian islands, the home of the Sirens, whose songs were so irresistibly seductive that seamen felt compelled to steer their ships towards the Sirens and the islands' rocks, and so met their doom. As his ship approached the islands, Odysseus instructed his crew (who had their ears plugged with beeswax) to tie him to the mast so he could hear the Sirens' song but resist its call. He also ordered his crew to ignore his pleas to be released. That turned out to be a good decision. When Odysseus heard the Sirens' song, he lost his mind and tried to break free, which would have meant his death. By sticking with his original plan, he survived.

Politicians see things a bit differently; they prefer discretion over rules—they hardly want to be tied to the mast. Political leadership is about making decisions, or about being perceived to be making decisions. The prevalent national and international funding model for a disaster response gives politicians plenty of opportunities: leaders can turn into benefactors, filling noisily presented begging bowls and spending the revenue at their discretion.

And, as was shown in Chapter 2, the evidence suggests that it pays politically to adopt this behaviour in both rich and poor countries. It is hard to believe, then, that politicians would want to give up this discretion. And yet in this book we are asking them to do just that to some extent because we want responses to disasters to be faster, more effective, and better coordinated, with less waste of lives and money. We argue that there are funding models that will make this possible, with pre-committed finance, not appeals. And for this, we want them to learn from Odysseus and be willing to commit to a plan, well before troubled times, and stick to it in their actions.

Why a plan? Because making better financing of disaster recovery possible requires knowing what has to be financed. So a sensible plan is needed: one that spells out what the risks are and who owns the risks, and clarifies the responsibility of local governments, the national government, international organizations, as well as families and firms themselves both during a crisis and during the recovery phase. It must be clearly stated who needs to do what to reduce the risks beforehand and how that will be enforced. Such a plan must appear reasonable and something that can actually be implemented. It must be general enough to be useful in a broad range of circumstances and yet specific enough to be credible. One condition for credibility is that the plan be underwritten—a realistic financing plan must be in place beforehand. And the financing of plans is only possible if there is a commitment to implementing the plan. It has to be a good plan, but just like in the *Odyssey* it needs a means of committing leaders to it.

The Politics of Credible Pre-Disaster Plans

Going down this route is not easy for politicians. Why be bound by plans and give up discretion? Why give up being a benefactor, not least because research has shown that the one who offers relief and support after disasters enjoys greater political clout? Even if much of the preparation is carried out beforehand, a disaster could unravel every carefully designed plan. In the highly charged political environment following a disaster, a plan is typically not sacrosanct—plenty of Sirens are making themselves heard. The plan then becomes just one of many inputs into a long, drawn-out negotiation among national and local governments, donors, business, and citizens over who will pay for what, when, and how.

There were plans in place when Hurricane Katrina reached New Orleans in 2005, but when the time came to implement them, the plans proved to be lacking shared commitments.[1] In the case of the 2015 Nepal earthquake, there was preparedness planning, but once the earthquake struck, logistical arrangements to get supplies in proved hard, while political disagreements slowed down responses.[2] Coordination was a challenge, and it reportedly took many months to reach a local political agreement on how to start allocating reconstruction funding.[3] If everybody knows a plan will be totally rewritten, then planning becomes a box-ticking bureaucratic exercise to ensure that there is something on paper in case anybody asks, even if everybody knows it carries no weight. What is required are plans that national and local politicians will commit to beforehand without risk of reneging afterwards.

The problem does not lie solely with national politicians. International humanitarian responses are based on need and need alone, an excellent moral principle, but one that tends to lead to responses based on plans prepared after a crisis has begun in which post-disaster needs are examined. Too often, much time is wasted by needs assessments and the slow negotiations among humanitarian and development organizations and with government over what the post-disaster need really is and what can be done. All the while the need is increasing, with people waiting, hungry, and homeless, and watching their jobs disappear. These types of plan prepared after disasters are not discussed here. Rather, we focus on planning for *possible* crises that will allow responses to become more predictable and to be financed beforehand.

In considering the type of planning described here, benefactors— governments, politicians, and humanitarian organizations—might give some thought to the costs of not planning. The absence of a plan and a serious commitment to act on it means there is little incentive to prepare for a disaster, resulting in a limited ability to respond quickly and not much urgency to invest beforehand in recovery and preparedness. And with limited planning, the immediate humanitarian response will lack coordination and effectiveness. Nurses, doctors, local officials, soldiers, and volunteers will devote all their energy to helping, but commitment alone cannot overcome operational failures. The costs of late responses are hard to quantify, but studies have suggested that half the caseload could have been avoided—equivalent to thousands of lives saved—if the Ebola response had arrived one month earlier.[4] And an early response to an Ethiopian drought would cost only a third of a full-fledged later response with the same impact.[5] Failures in response and recovery will ultimately also have a political cost.

So one needs to be able to offer an informed deal to those responsible across the world—locally, nationally, and internationally—to pre-commit to certain actions and responsibilities. One could think of it as an Odyssean pact, an agreement that binds all parties into the future to act in particular ways and avoids any discretion, despite its lure, to drop a plan when a disaster strikes. Benefactors should embrace ways to make big, showy *pre-disaster* promises and then tie themselves to the mast to ensure they deliver on what they have promised and stay far enough away from begging bowls and any over-involvement in post-disaster largesse. Benefactors could aim for *pre-disaster* political spoils and then *post-disaster* newspaper headlines that applaud a recovery planning system that works, a government and international community that have delivered on their promises—not headlines that announce new, ad-hoc post-disaster initiatives that do not add up.

But, like Odysseus, it is up to benefactors to choose whether they want to be tied up. This is an important political choice—not just a technical issue. To be willing to be tied up and move from begging-bowl financing to credible pre-disaster planning, benefactors will need to benefit politically from this move. And for it to be politically attractive, the recovery plan in question must be well prepared, feasible, and credible.

So how can benefactors extract pre-disaster spoils from credible pre-disaster plans? For one thing, they might recognize that many benefactors across the world, from governments to donors, are moving away from begging bowls. But how are they managing to sell this to their constituents, and why are some not managing to? The details vary, of course, from context to context, but what seems clear is that politically sellable solutions require a lot of collaborative preparatory work behind the scenes by men and women with at least four types of professional background.

The Scientists

Over the last few decades, scientists have made much progress in studying all kinds of hazards, such as extreme weather events and volcanic or seismic activity. Earthquakes are still largely not forecast, but volcanic eruptions can be forecast weeks in advance. Extreme weather events such as hurricanes and typhoons are increasingly being predicted some days or even a week ahead, offering valuable time to prepare. Slow-onset disasters such as droughts offer longer lead times because their impacts are felt months after the onset when harvests have to be collected or wells dry up. Monitoring of ocean temperatures, especially when the Pacific becomes exceptionally warm resulting in the disruptive force of the El Niño weather phenomenon, has allowed even earlier forecasts of possible droughts or floods. Early warning is in general something that will allow better responses to such events, even though early warning does not necessarily lead to early action.

This scientific progress feeds the pre-disaster planning process in a more fundamental way as well. Increasingly, scientists are able to offer more insight into what kinds of disaster could occur and with what likelihood. For example, an earthquake or extreme tropical cyclone may not have been seen in a century, but if it poses a very real catastrophic threat then the likelihood and potential impact need to be understood. Where the spread of exposed buildings or population increases the potential economic destruction that could be wreaked by an unfortunately placed disaster, this need is even stronger. Hazards are increasing because of climate change, and pandemics may be more of a threat in particular populations in densely populated areas.

Working across a vast array of disciplines, scientists have begun to develop risk models that offer a detailed understanding of how much damage or loss of life would be inflicted by various natural disasters and pandemics. This progress in modelling extreme events and their consequences has stemmed from thought experiments, careful observation, study of history, and advanced statistical analysis of data on the natural environment as well as economic, demographic, and social data. The resulting probabilistic models of natural-disaster events and pandemics and their consequences can help everyone understand what sorts of event could lead to disasters and need to be included in recovery plans.

Scientists have a further important role to play by laying out the odds of various events and scenarios and encouraging all to think carefully about them. For example, models could have predicted that an earthquake on the scale of the one that struck Nepal in 2015 or a pandemic that spirals out of control such as the Ebola virus that invaded West Africa in 2014 would have a reasonable probability of leading to large loss of life and economic damage. In playing that role, scientists can help to overcome decision-making behaviour more akin to that of gamblers, which is the curse of sensible disaster preparedness across all organizations. A gambler (and, let us be honest, many of us) often thinks luck in a game of chance will turn in his or her favour simply because there has been a particular series of bad outcomes—that is, in a coin-toss surely heads will come after a series of tails. However, this is a poor understanding of probability: the odds of getting heads in the next coin toss is not changed because it was preceded by a series of tails. The gambler's fallacy is a cognitive bias in which one tends to increase the perceived odds of events experienced more recently rather than form an unbiased assessment of all the risks.[6] Just as in most organizations, firms, or families, in governments the focus is often on the response to the previous disaster. The result is then perfect plans for recent past disasters and very poor plans for all the possible disasters that have a reasonable likelihood of happening.

Without scientists, one might expect a lot of plans across the world on how to deal with Ebola in West Africa and earthquakes in Nepal, whereas other infectious diseases or earthquakes may have very different patterns and impacts. This is a real and very visible risk at present: without scientists there will be an imbalance in what countries plan for.

That said, scientific knowledge alone is not enough. Communication of scientific findings at all levels of society is critical. If people do not understand the disaster risks to which they are exposed, being protected is not valued, and spending money on credible pre-disaster planning is not a vote-winner. Scientists need to help political leaders communicate clearly the risks faced and why investments should be made in reducing risks and responding better. Fixing this through visible, awareness-raising investments may support moves away from the begging bowl. This is easiest where local disasters are frequent and the threat of a natural disaster is part of the national psyche, as is the case for all of the countries we feature in this book.

The Bureaucrats

The central task of the women and men who work in national governments and international organizations tasked with disaster management is to undertake the preparation needed for a disaster response: to prepare policy that politicians may want to take forward, prepare a response plan, and prepare for recovery after a disaster. Drafting endless documents that lay all this out comes naturally to these officials—we know, we are two of them. But for the recovery plan proposed here, more is needed from bureaucrats: they need to be politically astute. Planning for a disaster is a political choice—not merely a technical exercise. Without something for their political masters to sell, there are no upfront political gains from credible planning, and so plans will not be pre-financed, let alone implemented. A technically sensible plan without political support or a budget is just a piece of paper.

Pulling Together the Parties

The main political decision to be made by all organizations with a stake in disasters is who will own what risk—that is, who will respond, how will they respond, and who will be responsible for paying what when a disaster occurs. National governments may claim they bear all the risks in their country; international organizations may claim they will respond on the basis of need and need alone. It is up to the officials in national governments and international organizations to turn these aspirations into affordable, implementable plans, with political backing. They can then help benefactors navigate the explicit political decisions to be made beforehand.

In fact, there are plenty of these kinds of decision. For example, in dealing with the economic damage after an earthquake or flood, should the national government protect all public infrastructure or only infrastructure owned by the national government? Will the national government contribute at all to the cost of protecting infrastructure owned by subnational governments? What happens when a subnational government will not pay its share—will the national government still pay its share? Will the national government contribute towards the cost of protecting low-income housing or agricultural production from disasters? Will homeowners or farmers have to pay for their share of protection to benefit from the government's contribution to protection? Who will be enrolled in a social safety net? Will there be targeting by community or by type of family? What can the ministry of finance actually afford? Will there be a focus on particular geographical areas or sectors of the economy? Of course, technical and financial analysis should inform these trade-offs, but ultimately they are political decisions.

Decisions also have to be made about the response to a public-health emergency in a poor country. Will the national government take charge and deal with the problem via the government-controlled health sector, or will it bring in private and charitable providers? Will government provide these other providers with resources? What will be the role of local governments versus the national government, and how will this role be financed? What will be the role of non-governmental organizations (NGOs)? Under what circumstances and conditions will the government call in the help of specialized international aid agencies? Will it hire more staff, and under what conditions? Will it compensate for economic losses from public-health measures? What is the role of the health ministry, the local communities ministry, and the ministry of finance, or indeed the presidency?

This decision making becomes even more challenging when more than one party is involved in financing or implementing a disaster response, because nobody likes to be coordinated. Given the economies of scale in financing and logistics, it is far, far better to have one well-coordinated plan than a large number of fragmented plans. Yes, there are substantial political and bureaucratic incentives to not work together—but, as discussed in Chapter 2, there is also strong evidence from evaluation of responses that not working together is costly for those exposed to disasters. A good plan should benefit from economies of scale in finance and logistics, and achieving this begins with the political and bureaucratic leadership. There has to be one joint political choice that all stakeholders are willing to buy into.

Having negotiations before a disaster over who will pay for what and who will do what is unlikely to be any easier than having the same negotiations after a disaster. However, postponement of hard choices only leads to strategic bargaining and costly delays after a disaster strikes. Before a disaster happens, there is a serious collective-action problem: many of the parties have little incentive to come to agreements in good time. Overcoming this collective-action problem is crucial to avoiding the serious coordination failures after the onset of a disaster. Therefore, astute officials are needed to steer all to negotiate and agree on good plans.

A good starting point for pre-disaster negotiation between parties is usually to think through who would be likely to do what in the event of a disaster—or who did what for a recent disaster. It may also be helpful to interview key informants to find out what each benefactor and each political constituency believe other benefactors would or should do in the aftermath of different kinds of disaster. For example, one might ask farmers, agribusiness leaders, other citizens, and civil servants in national and subnational agriculture and the finance ministry what they think government would do in the event of a catastrophic drought. One might also bring together nurses, doctors, community leaders, police officers, the military, ordinary citizens, NGO leaders, and different ministries to understand who they think would and should respond in a public-health emergency and how. In countries that plan well, the answers should be broadly consistent—citizens and subnational governments should know what they will be entitled to and benefactors should know what they are contributing to, but all too often these conversations do not take place or only with empty commitments and few consequences. It is, nevertheless, a crucial part of the process: without a clear factual understanding of who will do what and when, no sensible planning can take place. In countries that expect or have a history of outside support when disasters loom, it is critical to bring those outsiders into this pre-disaster negotiation.

Drawing Up the Plan

Skill in crafting a political statement is conducive to good planning. Many political statements about disaster risks undermine sensible planning. They focus on the inputs—that is, the people and resources one can mobilize, such as the contingency fund, officials, army, or some civil defence force; the vehicles and trucks available; the command and control structures needed to deploy them; the health services that can be on standby; and the supplies that can be requisitioned. This is a very natural way to plan, but by itself it tends not to work very well. Announcing what inputs they have at their disposal does not help bureaucrats know when to deploy them, how to target them, how to utilize them for disasters of different severities, or what to do for really big disasters when additional inputs are needed.

It is far better to start from outcomes, not inputs. This is the essence of being fully upfront about the ownership of the risks. Being clear about who and what needs to be protected—lives, health, livelihoods, assets, and infrastructure—gives financiers and implementers the space to arrange the logistics and structure the financing to achieve the outcomes.

A good plan, then, will be defined in a clear, public, joint declaration by all the relevant stakeholders who might contribute to post-disaster financing or implementation. The declaration will state who or what will be protected, against what, what (if any) conditions there will be for protection, how the protection will be implemented, and who will pay for what. Only after these aspects of the plan have been defined should the administrative, logistics, and financial specialists be brought in to fill in the technical details of the plan to achieve the stated outcomes.

Making it unambiguously clear who is responsible for what means clarifying what risks the national or local government will take on, and what risk have to be shared with households and firms. For example, a government has to state unequivocally whether it will cover all farmers if harvests fail, or just particular ones, and whether it expects others to insure themselves or cover their losses directly. A donor or multilateral agency may state outright that it will cover a particular share of the costs of scaling up a safety net; it may also declare that it will step in logistically if a national government obviously cannot handle a disaster. A global health organization may commit to deploy immediately if a particular infectious disease appears, or it may commit to enter to support the national government if after a specified number of days that disease is still spreading.

A good joint plan could start by declaring that the national and subnational governments will pay equal shares of the cost of reconstruction of subnational infrastructure damaged by a natural disaster, that reconstruction will 'build back better' to pre-agreed disaster-resilient building standards,[7] and that infrastructure will have to be registered to be eligible for the protection. Or a plan could declare that government and donors will use targeted cash transfers to jointly protect all households registered as living in a given area against drought-induced food insecurity (which the Hunger Safety Net Programme does in Kenya).

The Implementers

All this talk of science and planning may well drive those who work on the ground during crises to distraction. Heroic work is undertaken by all kinds of frontline workers during disasters: nurses, doctors, and community health workers; soldiers and civil defence workers; local officials and community leaders; staff from national and international NGOs; field staff of governments, donors, and international aid agencies; and vast armies of volunteers. Without their support and confidence, no plan can be implemented following a disaster.

As frontline workers, they are in the middle of the action when the suffering is at its worst, doing good where they can, driven by super-human energy, adrenaline, and moral commitment. They are crucial because they work with the people affected and listen to them. They are also the relayers of the bad news—of late response, poor coordination, and under-resourcing. The bureaucrats had better invite them in early on, as without their hard work but also their buy-in the best-written plan is just empty words.

The knowledge and experience of the implementers are central to understanding what can be done sensibly and in what order in the aftermath of a disaster. What relief will be needed in the weeks following the crisis? How will the reconstruction of lifeline infrastructure such as key bridges and hospitals work over the following months? And how should any subsequent reconstruction be sequenced? Any small or big plan should be tested by these implementers, including in practical exercises. How would it work? What are its strengths and weaknesses? How can it be improved?

During the drafting stages of plans, frontline workers will probably argue for adaptability and flexibility when circumstances change: a good plan will be clear on how it will evolve and change if required. They may also recommend decentralization so that decision making about support is carried out near the people in need. But evaluations and experience have also shown that simply leaving it to those on the ground to act as they see fit during crises does not necessarily lead to the best outcomes. Fragmentation and lack of coordination bedevil responses, as was discussed in Chapter 2. It is crucial, then, to settle beforehand on sensible plans and coordination mechanisms.

Finally, implementers can contribute significantly to improving response planning. There continues to be remarkably little evidence on the cost-effectiveness of the various response models in humanitarian support. During a drought or flood that has deprived people of their livelihoods, should one support families or target particular individuals? Should one focus on income support or targeted nutrition? One problem is that there are very few high-quality evaluations of humanitarian interventions in which hard data are collected early on in order to learn lessons for other crises.[8] Implementers can assist those trying to improve this situation, despite the difficulties of carrying out quality impact evaluations during the extreme circumstances of a disaster response.[9]

The Financiers

Finally, the financiers need to be invited to join the three other groups in the room. The men and women of finance are needed to work out how much different contingency plans would cost and to lock in agreements, so that the political agreement to a plan is tied to a credible commitment to finance the plan.

Trade-offs are always necessary when deciding who to protect and against what, and understanding the financial consequences of different plans for different potential disasters, the contingent liability, is critical. Actuaries and other financial types can use market-implied pricing techniques, now ubiquitous within insurance companies, to determine how much it will cost on average to finance a given contingent liability and therefore to implement a particular plan. These cost figures can support a virtuous circle between defining and refining the policy objectives, updating the plan, and estimating the cost of implementing the plan.

But putting a cost on potential political choices is not the only area in which financiers add value. Their real usefulness comes in making sure that promises are credible and will be kept. Political constituencies will need to know who will be protected once a disaster strikes and how, and for this to happen plans need to be locked down beforehand. It turns out that this takes quite a bit of subtle work behind the scenes.

According to contract theory in economics, merely having a contract is not enough unless its enforcement is beyond doubt: it has to be credible and designed so that no one can benefit by opting out of the agreement later and doing their own thing. Behavioural scientists point out that even if commitments are genuine and sensible, commitment devices (such as the mast to which Odysseus was tied) are required to ensure that commitments are actually kept, to avoid procrastination, and to make action as intended credible. The financiers should be on hand to tie Odysseus to the mast and to ensure that the other sailors do not respond to his call to be released when the Sirens call.

In practice, these solutions typically centre on financial contracts and budgetary mechanisms that are arranged before a disaster strikes to lock in the plan.[10] Done well, financial planning for disasters is not just about making sure that the money is available when it is needed; it is also the glue that holds all the pieces of the plan together and makes it credible (see Chapter 5). It ensures that funds are available quickly when—and only when—they are required by the plan, and it binds the various partners to pre-agreed objectives, decision processes, and implementation modalities to make the plan strong enough to withstand the whirlwind of highly charged post-disaster politics.

Avoiding Hot Air and Getting Results

Credible pre-disaster planning requires a lot of joint technical work from a variety of professionals. Without the scientists generating knowledge and the science communicators communicating it, nobody knows or cares about what disasters need to be planned for. Without the subtle manoeuvring of bureaucrats and officials to broker the different scenarios about who will have to bear what risk, coordinated declarations will not be politically attractive and plans will not be sustainably funded. Without the implementers and their critical voices, but also their commitment to certain actions and not others, contingency plans will not be sensible or logistically feasible. And without financiers able to apply know-how from insurance, declarations will just be hot air and serious planning will begin only after a disaster. This typically means coordination between government ministries and the full range of international development partners and multilateral institutions.

Tossing out the begging bowl and moving to credible pre-disaster planning requires all four types of professional working together, appreciating their place in the process, and delivering on their core responsibility. And it requires benefactors who are open to the idea of moving away from the old ways of doing things (see Chapter 4).

Given all this, it is perhaps unsurprising that the best disaster response systems are in countries where some of the professionals have an easy time. For example, Mexico issues about thirty disaster declarations every year, and empty promises from politicians about disaster responses are quite quickly shown for what they are. Voters have a pretty good understanding of disaster risk. International donors are not involved, and so the main issue is the coordination between the federal and state governments, and this has been tackled head on by the federal government, which became tired of being presented with thirty begging bowls a year by state governments. Research indicates that having reliable, timely access to post-disaster funding channelled through Mexico's FONDEN between 2004 and 2013 led to an increase in local economic activity between 2 and 4 per cent over the first year after a disaster—a big benefit.[11]

Embracing Pre-Disaster Planning

As soon as governments and their partners change their mindset, place themselves beyond the reach of the begging bowls, and opt for pre-disaster plans, planning starts making sense. Once the matching financial plans are on the table, it becomes really interesting. It is the time for some real political leadership, nationally and internationally, because the crucial endgame is nigh.

Plans cease to be beautiful fiction, based on an assumption of unlimited budgets and imaginary implementation capacity, and instead the process of planning forces governments and the international community to think through important political trade-offs *before* a disaster strikes. What or who can the ministry of finance actually afford to protect? If the implementation capability will be constrained (a city cannot be rebuilt in a day), how should the response be sequenced after a disaster? Should a government invest now in standby reconstruction capacity for rebuilding public structures, or register vulnerable people and their bank accounts so that cash transfers can be made quickly should a disaster strike? Should a government protect against only the really extreme disasters that are catastrophic at the national level, or also against the smaller, more localized disasters that can still devastate communities? Who should really be paying for their own protection, or at least contributing towards it? How much is the international community really able to contribute and for what? How will money flow to where the plan demands it—will it be routed through government or NGOs? What pre-disaster promises of protection are politically sellable (both in the country and to contributors to the humanitarian system) and affordable? Making these trade-offs is not easy, but the current system implicitly makes them, albeit hidden behind a lot of post-disaster razzle-dazzle, coordination failures, and delays.

Perhaps most importantly, credible pre-disaster financial planning can help to unblock chronic underinvestment in risk reduction. There are lots of reasons why municipal governments may underinvest in strengthening buildings, farmers may underinvest in new, more resilient crops or in drought- or flood-resistant seeds, and developers may build cities on earthquake fault lines. One reason may be that people believe—rightly or wrongly—that they will be bailed out when disaster strikes. Why should they then invest in risk reduction? Of course, one can blame the beneficiaries, but this is not a useful recipe for a solution. Solving this problem lies in reforming the role of the benefactor.

Benefactors can do more to promote sensible investments in risk reduction through a credible pre-disaster system of protection than through a discretionary begging-bowl system. For example, national governments can commit to contributing to the protection of municipal buildings, but only those that have undergone some minimum level of strengthening. Governments can subsidize the cost of insurance for farmers, but only for newer, more resilient crops or for farmers economizing on water use. Governments and donors can provide partial subsidies for homeowner earthquake insurance so that such insurance is affordable for all existing homes. For a new home built in a risky place, however, the cost of insurance will be commensurately greater. All of these approaches would encourage the beneficiary to invest in risk reduction.

Credible pre-disaster financing can also promote sensible investments by benefactors themselves in risk reduction. If a benefactor has 'owned up' to its contingent liability on its balance sheet, and if someone has a brilliant idea for how to invest now to reduce the cost of bearing that risk, the benefactor may be more willing to contribute some of its own money than if it was off balance sheet. For example, when national and subnational governments jointly agree on who is responsible for what reconstruction post-disaster, both are more inclined to invest in risk reduction. When governments and farmers agree to pay jointly for the cost of agricultural insurance, both have in interest in investing in climate-smart, resilient agriculture to reduce the insurance premium. The World Bank offers middle-income countries a line of credit, the Catastrophe Deferred Drawdown Option (Cat DDO), which can be drawn down by a national government within a day or two of a disaster resulting from a natural event. However, this programme is only available if a government makes specific policy reforms that enable or promote improved risk management in advance.

How to ensure that a plan is credible so that it will be implemented when a disaster hits is discussed in Chapters 4 and 5. But will politicians decide to trust the professionals and buy into the plan? Why should they? They know that being a benefactor and acting after a disaster strikes pays—the evidence tells them that approach is beneficial. So why trust a group of professionals and a plan? The best argument is that the evidence clearly indicates it is the best thing to do for people and countries when extreme events risk turning into disasters. Pre-disaster planning, when done carefully, would result in faster, more effective responses, and so can help avoid the kind of losses to people and economies documented in Chapter 2.

How convincing will all this be to politicians? Doing as we suggest will not lead to tangible outcomes because it is about economic losses avoided, about lives not lost or harmed. It is not about visibly rescuing people or about openly responding to petitions of support by local communities and authorities. Putting trust in pre-disaster planning may not lead to photo opportunities, to flag planting, or to patronage for the supporters of politicians, let alone electoral success—the evidence suggests it is unlikely to help with that. And, no doubt, there will be a class of politicians who will not want to budge if this is the price to be paid. Others will do it because the evidence tells them it is for the best for their country's citizens. In the end, then, pre-disaster planning is a political choice that politicians need to make, even if it ties their hands and even if it does not lead to tangible results they can exploit. And that is why politicians will have to act as leaders, doing what is best for their country's citizens and economy.

Recapping...

1. Good planning is based on an iterative dialogue among scientists, bureaucrats, implementers, and financiers about what or who is to be protected, how, and how much it will cost. Bad planning happens when at least one of these parties is missing from the dialogue.
2. Planning is a political choice; it is not just a technical exercise. A good plan will include a clear political statement before a disaster about who or what is to be protected, against what, what the conditions for protection are, and who will pay for the protection.
3. Political statements by governments or development partners about how much money would be made available or how many people would be mobilized in the event of a disaster are not conducive to good planning. Useful political statements focus on target outcomes and leave the details on the 'how' to be worked out by the implementing agencies and financiers.
4. Benefactors who want to maximize the development impact of their support should think through different natural disaster scenarios, assess what support they would provide in each scenario, and own up to this contingent liability when in discussions with other partners. A benefactor with either no contingency plan or its own stand-alone contingency plan will fall short in its efforts to help people.
5. Behavioural biases against good planning are strongest for the kinds of disaster that did not occur in the recent past—that is, for nearly all future disasters. To combat these biases, there is a particular need to invest in science-based risk information and clear communication of this information to ensure that everyone knows for which contingencies they need protection.

A Snapshot of the Literature

Credibly establishing risk ownership requires overcoming the pre-disaster collective-action problem in order to avoid serious post-disaster coordination failures. Clear risk ownership is a basic tenet of sound risk management (World Bank 2014b). It is recognized as a fundamental principle of enterprise risk management (Nocco and Stulz 2006; Lam 2014) and is widely acknowledged as important for sound disaster risk management (UNISDR 2011; World Bank 2014a), including pandemic risk management (WHO 2015). The need for cross-disciplinary teamwork for complex but effective resilience-building solutions is also well understood (World Bank 2013).

Hsiang and Narita (2012) analyse the deaths and damages arising from tropical cyclones worldwide for the period 1950–2008 and find that countries with more frequent tropical cyclones suffer lower losses from similar events, suggesting that adaptation and risk reduction are more successful in these countries. Ley-Borrás and Fox (2015) have compiled an overview of the generation and uses of disaster risk information for financial protection solutions.

In the literature on humanitarian relief networks, Stephenson (2005) presents an overview of the issues, challenges, and possible solutions related to post-disaster humanitarian assistance. In particular, Stephenson argues that effective coordination among aid agencies is hampered by competition for clients, disparate organizational structures, the need to attract media attention, and the costliness of coordination efforts. He suggests changing their organizational cultures to encourage operational coordination. Janssen et al. (2010) and Bharosa et al. (2010) find that relief workers are often more concerned with receiving information from others than giving information to others who may benefit, and that understanding each other's work processes is crucial to improving coordination. In a similar spirit, Kapucu (2006) argues that in order to ensure effective communication at the time of a disaster, organizations should establish inter-agency communication before disasters strike.

There is a rich literature on emergency logistics, including pre-disaster operations such as evacuation, facility placement, and stock pre-positioning, and post-disaster operations such as relief distributions and casualty transportation. The collection of essays in

Christopher and Tatham (2014) stresses the importance of sharing information in order to put in place agile, synchronized supply networks. Van Wassenhove (2006) calls for stronger partnerships between the public and private sectors for managing post-disaster logistics. Caunhye et al. (2012) take a look at the literature on optimization models in emergency logistics, and Zeimpekis et al. (2013) provide an overview of recent research results and future trends in operational research for disaster relief.

4

PLANNING FOR DISASTER RECOVERY

Changing the default setting

A to Samual Mengisha speaks proudly about the Gebrale Iddir, the funeral society of which he is the secretary, in the village of Bukicho in the southern highlands of Ethiopia. The society was founded about twenty years ago, and his family has been a member ever since. Life is still hard for the families in this village, which is dependent on rain-fed agriculture, growing *enset* (false banana), coffee, and maize. In the area, funerals are expensive and rather too common.

Although conditions have definitely improved in recent years, more than a third of the families are classified as not having enough resources for their basic needs, and in a village like this, about one in ten children does not survive past the age of 5. Just as everywhere across the world, providing a decent burial for a deceased family member is important. Relatives and friends are invited to share their grief. Hospitality in the form of food and drink plays a big part in a dignified burial. Community cohesion is such that relatives of the deceased can rely on support from others in this time of need, but, still, not being able to pay for a funeral when required is sad and shameful.

This *iddir* has fifty-four members. Every year, members pay a membership fee of about US$5, either in instalments or in one go; new members pay an entry fee of $4 as well. When a member or the spouse of a member dies, the society pays out $12 to the family in cash—a smaller sum if another close relative dies. Contributions are predictable, and so members can plan carefully to ensure they have the cash rather than being surprised when a sudden death requires extra cash. Ways to raise extra emergency cash—again before the pot is empty—are specified. At the time of the conversation with Ato Samual, the *iddir* had cash reserves of about $290. It also owned a canvas tent, plates, and glasses worth about $200, which members brought along to a funeral.

Ethiopia has tens of thousands of *iddirs* that operate like this. Typically, they have fewer than 100 members. Probably originating in the Gurage communities, the *iddir* model can now be found across Ethiopia, even in urban areas and among civil servants, teachers, and World Bank employees in their Addis Ababa office. Contributions vary, but everywhere the rules are very similar. Membership is select-ive, and an entry fee is payable. A group usually holds the reserves in cash or buys some assets. *Iddirs* are considered an essential part of the Ethiopian cultural fabric. Many of these funeral societies in Ethi-opia are expanding to take on other risks such livestock death or illness. Essentially, they can be thought of as mutual societies, histor-ically at the root of some of the largest insurance companies in the world.[1]

As noted in Chapter 2, similar groups can be found elsewhere—for example, in India, Tanzania, and South Africa.[2] They offer a sensible solution to a problem. A delay in finding the resources for an uncer-tain event such as a funeral is stressful and wastes time, and so organizing financing beforehand is one part of the solution. It also helps that the response by the group is well defined: a pre-determined cash transfer plus some practical assistance to help with the funeral. And the simple and clear decision rules for implementation help to make it functional. In fact, this is small-scale risk management that works for rich and poor alike: those wanting bigger funerals either set up groups with higher fees and payouts, or, more commonly, join multiple groups so they can receive multiple payouts to finance a more expensive funeral.

Meanwhile, there are no opportunities for procrastination, for strategic behaviour, or for benefactor behaviour. In fact, *iddirs* have group incentives to ensure that disasters are avoided—that is, for risk reduction. Because they can force all members to attend meetings or take part in specific activities as part of their membership, and because it is in their collective interest to limit mortality, they are proving to be excellent vehicles for spreading health education and other developmental messages.

Why aren't similar principles applied to managing disasters across the world? Of course, the problems that arise when a sudden death occurs in a village are far smaller than when a disaster strikes. Lots of people are affected at the same time, and planning for large-scale disasters and the decision making required for preparation and responses are far more difficult. But some of the principles are very similar, whether one is dealing with a community planning sensibly for burial support or a national government or international organization preparing a credible response to a possible disaster.

The Flaws of Human Decision Making

At the heart of any credible pre-disaster plan is a system for post-disaster decision making. Decision making is hard, even if the political will is there. However, if the system for decision making is well thought through, it will serve as a basis for a viable alternative to discretionary begging-bowl financing. If it is not, it is back to the begging bowls.

In recent decades, research in psychology and behavioural economics has illuminated the flaws of human decision making, but also what to do about them. Three related lessons from this behavioural science research can help in the design of better decision-making systems to cope with disasters. The first lesson is that people tend to place too little value on the future; they have a bias towards the present day instead. The result is that they are not inclined to act now for future benefit, even if there is plenty of evidence of regret afterwards. An example is not saving enough for retirement—and, indeed, not protecting oneself against potential future harm.[3] To overcome this bias, people can use commitment devices to lock themselves into certain actions. Odysseus understood that, and he found a way to pre-commit to certain actions by tying himself to the mast and avoiding the song of the Sirens. Poor Ethiopians have clearly found another way by paying a regular contribution to a fund that can be used to pay for funerals.[4]

The second lesson is that people tend not to change what they are doing unless the incentive to do so is strong—the 'status quo bias'.[5] Inertia and procrastination go hand in hand with this bias: inaction tends to be preferred over action. Businesses and governments have begun to discover they can exploit this human tendency by making the choice for clients or constituents (such as enrolment in a pension scheme) and then forcing them to opt out if they disagree with that choice. There is strong evidence that if action has to be taken to opt out rather than opt in, enrolment in pension schemes increases dramatically.[6] In general, changes in the default setting has proved to be an effective strategy for nudging people towards better outcomes, and it is now recognized as one of the primary routes through which behavioural science is informing public policy.[7]

The third lesson builds on the finding that people tend to have limited information-processing capacities, which affects the quality of their decision making, even when the stakes are high.[8] Behavioural scientists have suggested that much can be gained from keeping things simple: ensure that plans and any decision making they entail are kept as clear and simple as possible. Well-designed, intelligent decision rules and triggers will make the difference.[9] So for funerals, whereas different people may have different financial needs, different mortality risks, or different desires for simple or extravagant funerals, the *iddirs* have only one fixed contribution for all members and one fixed payout when a member dies. This is not necessarily the best possible outcome for all members, but a simple, clear set of decision rules allows this group to function and to function well.

It Isn't Rocket Science (or Is It?)

So, what does this mean for decision making around disasters? It suggests the need for a clear-cut, straightforward disaster response plan that can be easily implemented. Strong commitment devices should be found to ensure that the tendency to resort to the default setting of inaction is changed to one of action. Clear-cut triggers and decision rules will aid decision making. It is not rocket science—in fact, it is probably more difficult than that; it is about human behaviour, not Newton's laws, and there are far more unknowns. Any extreme event that may lead to a disaster will happen in very specific circumstances involving many people whose actions and reactions are not easily predicted. How then does one make effective decisions on launching a successful response?

No one has either the time or the imagination to plan fully for everything that would have to happen after any disaster, so some post-disaster discretion will always be needed. The questions to be answered here are these: What should be decided before a disaster, and what should be decided afterwards? What should be on standby, ready for take-off, at all times, and what can be decided later?

One option would be to prepare rough plans for the people or buildings that will be protected in a disaster, how they will be protected, and who will pay for it. Then, after the disaster, a group of experts, bureaucrats, or political leaders would quickly work out the details of the response. The problem with this approach is that in a highly charged post-disaster environment, there *will be* negotiation over the details of how the money will flow and to whom, and there *will be* procrastination while waiting for more information. All this will take time. Strategic discretion is the enemy of speed, particularly after a big disaster, and particularly in an environment rife with benefactors, begging bowls, and bureaucracies. Around the world, there is no shortage of pre-disaster plans laying out the principles for who is supposed to make what decisions when, but again and again that information does not lead to timely action—it just provides ammunition for long, drawn-out negotiations. It will not get the response off the ground in time.

Instead of governments and their partners making approximate commitments, roughly agreeing to everything that will happen in the months after a disaster, they could take some lessons again from the Gebrale Iddir. It does not offer a full response plan for everything that happens after the death of a member. Rather, it provides precisely defined support in cash and in kind under specific circumstances, with all the financing sorted out beforehand. In general, it is more useful for governments and their partners to make precise, focused commitments to a credible set of minimal actions that pre-identified implementers have the authority and financing to undertake immediately. These actions would be financed and implemented based on pre-agreed rules and triggers, without the need for any begging bowls or any further green light from political masters. This precise, immediate action plan would define what data would be collected on day one and what financing and actions they would automatically trigger; what data would be collected on day two and how they could accelerate or decelerate actions, etc. The idea is similar to a launch sequence: over time the data force a (minimal) sequence of actions taken in line with a predefined timetable.

The plan could be as simple as providing fast cash or food transfers to drought-affected people. Such a response would require some investments beforehand in identifying the vulnerable households and categorizing them by level of vulnerability, and it would require agreeing beforehand to the rainfall patterns or satellite data that would automatically trigger food or cash support to households. If a drought is mild, perhaps only the most vulnerable households would receive support, but for a more extreme drought support could automatically be extended to less vulnerable households as well. Government or its partners could always provide top-up support over and above this minimal response on a discretionary basis, but the minimal response would be planned for and financed in advance of any possible drought and would happen automatically.

Or the plan could simply apply to the reconstruction of government-owned infrastructure following an earthquake. Before any earthquake, the 'lifeline' infrastructure (such as key roads, bridges, or hospitals) could be identified and prioritized as part of the pre-disaster plan, and the implementing agency responsible for post-disaster reconstruction of this infrastructure would be identified. Immediately after an earthquake of a given magnitude and epicentre, a pre-agreed budget would automatically be made available to the implementing agency for reconstruction of this lifeline infrastructure. The implementing agency would be responsible for immediately launching reconstruction of the lifeline infrastructure, using the initial budget and applying the pre-agreed principles for prioritizing reconstruction to the specific details of the earthquake.[10]

An earthquake could also trigger an additional budget for a detailed, objective assessment of the full extent of the damage for all lifeline infrastructure. Such an assessment would automatically unlock additional budgetary funds if the initial automatic budget turned out to be insufficient, so that all lifeline infrastructure is in full working order within six months of any earthquake. Planning for a disaster might also include provision for the implementing agency responsible for post-disaster reconstruction to invest in reconstruction capabilities, develop and implement procurement pre-qualification criteria, and sign retainer agreements with construction companies to ensure that the country has the capacity within the construction sector to respond adequately to an earthquake.

This does not mean delegating all post-disaster decision making to technical agencies and replacing all post-disaster discretion with pre-agreed rules and objective triggers. We are merely proposing that a credible, rules-based plan that everyone knows will be implemented be in place, based on an agreement made before the disaster about who or what will be protected, how the protection will work, and who will pay.

In countries that have taken this approach, a concise, credible plan changes the default setting for responding to disasters from 'wait and see' to 'implement what is in the plan'. This approach may not be perfect, but it sidesteps the delays and warped incentives of the begging bowl. And if this immediate response plan is well constructed, it will allow timely, sensible actions.

All Systems Go

A rocket launch sequence needs to culminate in take-off, and that is possible with a precise countdown and a set of predefined systems that ensures that all systems are go. In the same way, certain decision-making and implementation systems need to be in place before a disaster to ensure a response plan can be implemented.

A *clear command and control system* for strong leadership of the post-disaster response is required for plan implementation. All too often, poor coordination post-disaster hampers responses. Implementers can provide helpful input on how command and control of implementation should work, and how, at the technical level, different implementing agencies can work together towards common goals. All parties should agree on a coordination system, and that can only be done beforehand.

Information systems that can be scaled up quickly during crises are essential to the implementation of response plans. They can then relay information to the coordinators and allow plans to be adapted to actual need. But this will only work and will not unravel carefully prepared and balanced plans if clear decision rules are made beforehand on when and how to use the information. During the 2014 Ebola outbreak in West Africa, coordination as well as good data from the ground were crucial for an effective response: without good knowledge of where the pandemic had spread and who had been in contact with the sick and the dead, no effective response was possible. Similarly, without good data on where communities are cut off and what is required to re-establish infrastructure after flooding or an earthquake, those implementing a response plan will move resources to the wrong places.

Scalable delivery systems to reach poor and vulnerable populations after a disaster are also essential. Setting up the logistics for delivering food or health care after disasters requires considerable planning beforehand. Instead of establishing new delivery structures, governments might find that a much more promising route is to build a disaster response into the existing systems. Increasingly, even poor countries have developed rather well-functioning social-protection mechanisms, targeting poor and vulnerable households. The idea is to have these systems ready at all times to expand quickly to reach more people or to implement higher levels of transfers. Such *shock-responsive social protection* could provide the institutional structures needed to reach the poor and vulnerable quickly and at scale.[11]

During 'normal' circumstances, these schemes tend to be relatively well defined—for example, Ethiopia's Productive Safety Net Programme (PSNP) covers many millions of food-insecure people in normal circumstances. As part of the disaster-preparedness plan, one could take all the steps needed beforehand to allow this scheme to expand at scale—both in terms of giving higher payouts to already enrolled people and in terms of expanding the scheme to other pre-defined groups that now are vulnerable. This possibility is present in the PSNP. This is also the principle underlying Kenya's Hunger Safety Net Programme: it can expand when a drought occurs, using a pre-defined trigger. Similar arrangements could be made for other essential services during a crisis, such as expanding public health or WASH (water, sanitation, and hygiene) interventions during crisis situations, not in an improvised way but in one planned ahead of time. And there are alternatives or additions to cash transfer schemes if the circumstances allow: for example, populations may be covered by subsidized agricultural or homeowners' disaster insurance.

After a disaster strikes, much humanitarian support is often delivered in kind, such as food, but evidence suggests that this is frequently not the best response.[12] Trying to deliver food directly to people is costly and logistically demanding. Often during disasters, even when there are droughts or harvest failures in particular areas, the overall food supplies per se are not the problem. The more cost-effective, more transparent, and faster alternative is to ensure that vulnerable populations are offered income support—cash—so they can afford to buy the food and other essentials they need. However, markets must also be monitored to ensure that they are functioning and well stocked. With today's technology, cash can be sent to vast numbers of people via mobile phones and other methods, which makes cash transfers even faster and more transparent than people procuring and delivering goods. The typical current default in delivering support is to deliver it in kind. Changing the default setting by always delivering cash unless there is an explicit rationale not to do so would be consistent with the evidence.[13]

Lessons from Insurance

At this point, a plan is in place, and systems are ready to deliver at scale when required. But how will those implementing the plan ensure it will happen—that is, how will they make sure there is take-off when the launch sequence is completed? Is it possible to design objective triggers that are both reliable and trustworthy? And, above all, can the data system that drives decisions be both difficult to 'game' and sensible? These requirements raise many additional questions. As for gaming, is it possible to know that the data really are objective and trustworthy? Can people manipulate the data system in their favour? As for being sensible, does the system strike an appropriate balance between accuracy, timeliness, and cost? That question, in turn, raises other considerations: Is the system accurate enough to be used to trigger post-disaster action? What is the likelihood of it misfiring, either triggering when it should not or not triggering when it should? Is the system timely enough? Does it strike the right balance between early, approximately targeted action and later, more precisely targeted action? Finally, how much will the data system itself cost?

These are the very questions that insurers grapple with when they sign disaster insurance contracts. Therefore, those designing good triggers to induce action by governments or international organizations could learn a few lessons from them. As insurers know all too well, as soon as the data begin to drive decisions and financial flows, there will be attempts to manipulate or falsify the data—for example, to make a fraudulent claim that a home was damaged by a flood even though it was not. Or a poorly designed system could incite some people to become negligent about reducing their risk to disasters—an issue known as 'moral hazard'. For example, they might not adopt basic flood protection measures because they know their insurance will cover any loss. Moral hazard, as characterized by economists, is not a moral judgement on the behaviour of an individual in a system; it is a judgement on the system itself. If farmers can receive more money from insurers, government, or donors when they underinvest in risk reduction or adaptation to climate change, there is something wrong with the system. If governments can get more money from donors or the international humanitarian system or indeed insurance companies if they underinvest in resilience, there is also something wrong with the system.

A credible system, then, has to be based on credible data. After a flood, how does the national government know whether a school has actually been damaged, whether a farmer has actually lost her harvest, or whether a homeowner has actually lost his home? How does the government ensure that people are not fiddling with the data to get more support than they should? If the data that drive post-disaster decisions are discretionary, then the system is discretionary. Credible data are needed on damage and loss, or at least on credible proxies for these, and that means investing in data systems, people, and processes before a disaster to ensure that after the disaster the money flows to where it is needed. In short, the data have to be objective and protected from meddling, and the system must be structured in a way that does not give people incentives to change their behaviour pre-disaster to game the system.

A decision system also must be based on the right data, striking a sensible balance between timeliness, accuracy, and cost. In the

Box 4.1: Three Rules-Based Approaches Used by Insurance Companies to Assess Damage and Loss from a Disaster

Individual Loss Adjustment

Most traditional insurance contracts are indemnity-based—that is, what triggers a payout is a loss, and the insurance indemnifies the policyholder against the loss. In practice, that means the insurance company has to send a certified loss adjuster who assesses objectively the actual damage for each insured farm, building, or injured person, which is costly, or it has to trust the information provided by the policyholder, which may not be trustworthy.

This process typically does not work very well for disasters because, first, it takes time to assess individually each insured object or person affected by the disaster to confirm that a falsified claim was not submitted; and, second, the process opens the door to moral hazard—for example, a farmer does not work as hard on her farm because she knows that if the crop fails during a drought the insurer will pay. An insurer may respond to such a possibility by adding lots of conditions to contracts. For example, a contract may specify that drought-resistant seed must be used and pesticide must be applied to insured crops.

Area Average Index

For a given area, an insurer can estimate the average damage to farms, buildings, or people by either calculating and summing all the individual damage or using the power of statistical sampling. The insurance payout rate for everyone insured in that area would then be the same. This 'area average index' approach can be much cheaper than an individual loss adjustment and can substantially reduce the moral hazard because no one person can influence the index. For example, the average crop yield in a subdistrict as measured by a series of statistical samples of crop yields might yield a reasonable estimate of how much farmers in the subdistrict have suffered from drought, and no individual farmer would be able to substantially influence the index.

The advantage of such indexes is that, by design, they are not sensitive to the behaviour of individuals (thereby reducing the moral hazard), and the information on which they are based can be collected in ways that make them difficult to manipulate (thereby reducing the potential for fraud). Their big disadvantage is that they do not capture the

(continued)

heterogeneity of impact within the area—a tropical cyclone, say, may have damaged only some buildings in the area, but insurance based on indexes treats all buildings as though they had the same severity of damage. And such an index can be quite expensive to implement because it requires a sampling frame and audited loss adjustment.

Parametric Index
In this different type of index-based insurance approach, payouts are based on parametric triggers that are *correlates* of losses, not individual or area average losses themselves. For example, satellite data on rainfall or the blueness of the ground might serve as a reasonable proxy for the degree of flooding, or data on ground acceleration from an earthquake monitoring station might be a reasonable proxy for the destructive power of an earthquake. These policies offer a big advantage: when a serious event happens, there is no costly verification and typically no need for anyone to even travel to the disaster-affected area to conduct a loss adjustment.[1] As a result, payouts can be very fast and there is little room for fraudulent manipulation. The main disadvantage of such an approach, as a type of index insurance, is the risk that a payout is not made even though a loss has occurred and the risk that a payout might be made even though there is no loss.

[1] There are exceptions—for example, for rain gauges or river flow stations that have to be read manually. However, even these are increasingly automated.

immediate aftermath of a disaster it may be that only quite crude information is available to drive decisions, but over time more accurate information can be usefully collected to refine and better target later, complementary responses.

Insurance companies have struggled with this problem for decades and have come up with three rules-based approaches for trying to capture whether a person or building has suffered damage from a disaster while also trying to economize on the cost of information. Described in Box 4.1, these approaches are the individual loss assessment, the area average index, and the parametric index.

How do these three types of data rank in terms of cost, accuracy, and speed? Typically, the individual loss adjustment is the most expensive and the slowest; the area average index is in the middle on both counts; and the parametric is the least expensive and fastest. However, the order is reversed when it comes to accuracy, with individual loss adjustment on top, followed by the area average index and then the parametric index.

Applying Rules-Based Approaches to Disaster Planning

The three approaches described in Box 4.1 are also the right ones to consider when thinking about developing data systems that will provide a foundation for automated specific response plans. In some cases, a crude individual loss assessment, such as targeting all those displaced or all those with a collapsed roof or flooded home, may be quite effective. The data system underlying this approach would have to operate much like loss adjustment works for individual indemnity insurance.

This approach requires a system for individual loss adjustment and auditing, as well as trained adjusters. Otherwise, the response might be too slow, or it might be manipulated by those on the ground. Some conditions may also have to be set for protection, such as requiring that a building satisfy a certain building code. In most post-disaster situations, however, the default setting should not be requiring implementing agencies to wait for a full comprehensive assessment of damage or loss. Rather, the response should be designed to evolve as new data become available. Where early action is important, as it usually is, triggers should be based on index insurance products (area average or parametric indexes, depending on the relative cost, speed, and accuracy). The use of clear and transparent triggers based on the information that is immediately available (and not with long delays on losses linked to data collection) could serve as a kind of triage for prioritizing response. Actions, then, would be based on forecast rainfall or harvest failures, the distance to the epicentres of earthquakes and their magnitude, or the number of cases of a serious infectious disease.

These triggers could build on the data generated by the existing early warning systems, which are much better than they used to be. For example, better information is available on hydro-meteorological systems and their likely consequences, including their impacts on harvests, flooding, or cyclones; slow-onset disasters can be better predicted, including links to famine or public-health problems; and even early warning systems for rapid-onset disasters such as earthquakes and tsunamis are in place in some countries and are getting better.[14]

It is important to continue to improve early warning systems, but by themselves they are by no means sufficient for good decision making. An early warning is of limited use if the main response, especially support for reconstruction and for protecting livelihoods, is always late. The longer the wait after a disaster, the easier it is to justify a need, but acting early is typically much more cost-effective. For example, reports of Ebola circulated for many months before any kind of serious international action was taken.[15] Similarly, drought in some areas in the Horn of Africa and East Africa was reported in 2011, many months before the world took notice and began to respond.[16] To work as an index insurance product, a trigger should not lead to a set of options for a decision-making body; it should result in an automatic decision. In other words, a defined set of indicators reaching particular pre-agreed values should lead to a defined action, as in insurance. Early warning systems would turn into early action systems.

Other monitoring data can also be useful when contemplating action. Some observers have claimed that the Ebola outbreak was subdued not only by social mobilization but also by careful information gathering and processing (such as incidents of unsafe burial or rumours of hidden cases) that received an immediate response. Similarly, there is good evidence that in the 2005 Kashmir earthquake systematic information platforms such as RISEPAK offered live updates on where the needs were throughout a long period, thereby improving the effectiveness of the response.[17] Thanks to the advances in satellite imaging and social media and in other digital areas, systematic information gathering is now considerably easier, but planning beforehand on how to use it and what information will trigger specific action is important. And some data systems, such as those for national health and nutrition surveillance data, are still quite expensive and will take many years to build.

User-generated data are, of course, susceptible to fraudulent manipulation, and so by themselves are not useful as a trigger for financing. However, they could still be used as part of a rules-based system for action, in particular for guiding when to collect the data needed for more accurate but expensive back-up triggers. For example, suppose a government wants to protect farmers against a severe loss in crop production and chooses to do so using a combination of a trigger based on rainfall and a back-up trigger based on an area average yield index. If the area average yield index is quite expensive to calculate, the government could decide whether to collect the data for a back-up trigger using a cellphone survey that indicated it had been a very bad crop year—a situation not being picked up by the rainfall trigger.

Rules and triggers also can be applied to early action, recognizing that no early-action rule can be perfect. It is inevitable that a response will be too late for some droughts and too early for others. But a rule for early action does not have to be perfect to be better than waiting— it just has to be good enough. And the science of droughts is certainly good enough to ensure that early action is better than waiting.

In fact, providing cash or food to households early in the face of an ensuing drought seems to be much more cost-effective for reducing food insecurity than waiting until the drought is in full swing. In the Horn of Africa and pastoral areas of East Africa, the rainy season in early 2011 failed, and the rains the previous year had also been poor, so substantial hardship could be expected. Nevertheless, several months passed before a response began, leading to delays in reaching people.[18] A more appropriate response would have been to trigger at least some actions as soon as it became clear that the rains were poor, several months earlier, even though farmers still had reserves by then. In that case, help could have been on the ground much more quickly, pre-empting difficulties (and benefiting from much cheaper operations).

Reconstruction of damaged lifeline infrastructure such as hospitals and key roads after a large earthquake is another area that could benefit from agreement before a disaster on an objective, transparent, independent, manipulation-resistant procedure for determining the damage and rules for determining who will pay for reconstruction. And yet this crucial work is often delayed because after a disaster different parts of government are negotiating over the total cost of the damage and who will pay.

Just as it is for disaster insurance, the heart of a minimal response plan will always be the data. If the data are too easy to manipulate, too costly, too slow, or too unreliable, the system will not be politically sustainable. And just as for insurance, getting it right will require investing in systems and people before disasters, so that the data-collection process can run smoothly during and in the aftermath of a disaster. Good data will be at the core of any attempt to change the default setting from inaction to action because they will give credibility to the decision rules required.

For Benefactors, a New Strategy

Benefactors who care about the impact of their financial support should be willing to settle for a new decision-making system. Instead of waiting for the appearance of begging bowls after a disaster, benefactors could agree to commit the majority of their funds to financing the planning, preparation, and implementation of the coordinated default response to a disaster as described in the response and recovery plan. It would not be a vague, unwieldy plan, but a pre-agreed, coordinated plan with a specific, defined set of actions to which they would commit.

To make this work, discretion needs to be replaced by rules to guide decision making—that is, triggers for action and a credible commitment.

It will help to overcome procrastination and inertia, the enemies of fast decision making. In the process, many of the bureaucratic or political incentives for inaction will disappear. And moving from post-disaster discretion towards pre-disaster rules can help to clarify ownership of the risk—who is responsible for what—and this can promote good incentives for investments in preparedness and risk reduction and avoid regret afterwards.

Even when decision making is governed by decision rules and algorithms and early warning leads automatically to early action, there is still ample room for political leadership. It is not about the computers taking over, generating triggers to which one needs to respond without judgement. It is about changing the default setting. Instead of inaction and the status quo being the default, triggers will start actions, and policymakers will need to act *to stop* action.

Leaders of national governments and international organizations would then have *to justify* why they stopped or changed their early action systems from being implemented in, say, a drought. In the recent Ebola outbreak, for example, slow decision making and delayed declaration of an emergency were generally acknowledged to have caused loss of life and hardship for many. The approach to a disaster response we propose would have changed the dynamic of the decision making, putting a focus on *stopping* action if leaders had so wished. During a drought, a response would also be triggered automatically—for example, based on harvest forecasts from weather data. Leaders could stop the response, but they would no doubt be cautious in doing so.

As plans are implemented, new data become available, and further actions and course corrections are triggered, leaders will need to keep everyone on board and hold the course. They will need to show concern and commitment to all those affected, communicate what is being done to all involved, and coalesce all in the mission to deliver. No pre-agreed plan, no rules will be perfect. There will be times when triggers fail or are imprecise. Leaders will need to judge information on unforeseen matters, justify any deviations from plans, and act accordingly, without allowing special interests to take over and game the system.

The result of this new approach will be the emergence of a new accountability during disasters. Meanwhile, leaders can take political credit for implementing the plans to which they previously agreed. Yes, they can overrule systems, but they can expect to be judged for deviations from agreed plans.

Recapping...

1. By ensuring that as little as possible must be decided by stakeholders when a disaster strikes, rules can promote decisive, timely action.
2. A rules-based system is only as good as the data that drive it. The data need to be resistant to manipulation and strike the right balance between cost, speed, and reliability.
3. Any data that could trigger action will depend on investments before a disaster in design of the data-collection system, including an audit function, and in the human and technological capacity to collect data in a timely manner.
4. Three types of data are particularly useful for triggering post-disaster action: ground data on the damage to or losses of people and buildings, area average index data on damage and losses, and parametric indexes.
5. No rule is perfect, and so there should be some discretionary back-up system to deal with situations in which the rules fail.
6. Benefactors should channel their financial support into precise sets of plans in which it is clear who exactly is being protected, how, and who is paying.

A Snapshot of the Literature

Early behavioural economics literature provides strong motivation for considering simple plans. Simon's *Rational Choice and the Structure of the Environment* (1956) hypothesized that human beings have limited cognitive capacities, and therefore simple approaches may be more effective than technically first best approaches that are not sufficiently well understood. One implication is that using simple algorithms and clear decision rules will improve decision making (Gigerenzer and Goldstein 1996). For example, in medicine the use of checklists in diagnosis has contributed to much better diagnosis and treatment (Pronovost et al. 2006; Gawande 2010). Clear heuristics also help to overcome confirmation bias when relying on experts. This bias is the tendency to search for or interpret information in a way that confirms one's preconceptions, leading to statistical errors.

Rational decision making is also affected by other cognitive biases (for an introduction, see Kahneman 2011). Present bias is the tendency to over-value immediate rewards at the expense of long-term intentions. It can lead to procrastination—situations in which the current self defers decisions towards some long-term goal while planning for some future self to pursue it. Hyperbolic preferences can be used to model this behaviour, which is called time-inconsistent and leads to regret (as the future self will have wanted the current self to have acted differently). O'Donoghue and Rabin (1999) discuss such preferences in more detail. Present bias may be overcome using commitment devices and other ways to increase self-control. Thaler and Bernatzi (2004) show how 'Save More Tomorrow' can overcome lower pension savings because of the present bias caused by limited self-control. The essence of the programme is straightforward: people commit in advance to allocating a portion of their future salary increases towards retirement savings. Ashraf et al. (2006) found that commitment savings products can increase savings for people who may display present bias in the Philippines.

Another bias affecting decision making is status quo bias, a preference for the current state of affairs, even if there would be gains from change (Samuelson and Zeckhauser 1988). Loss aversion is a possible explanation (Kahneman et al. 1991). Overcoming status quo bias is possible through changes in the default option, such as automatically enrolling workers in pension schemes and making them act to leave the scheme rather than making them act to join. Madrian and Shea (2001) show how changing this default increases the uptake of retirement savings products in a context in which too little retirement savings take place.

At the level of governments, time-inconsistent preferences have also been observed. It is well recognized that governments are often tempted not to do what they said they would do, or do things now that later on they will regret. This time inconsistency can often benefit from institutional designs that make government's announcements credible. For example, a credible commitment to a monetary policy rule, such as the Taylor rule (Taylor 1993), could perform substantially better than a discretionary approach in which government is given full discretion at every moment in time (Lucas 1976; Kydland and Prescott 1977). This insight led to central banks being given some degree of political independence over monetary policy, so that they can operate under clear rules and not the discretion of political leaders.

Time inconsistency problems in public policy appear in a range of situations. For example, in developing countries a government is unable to make a commitment to private firms that, if they invest in public infrastructure such as a water or electricity distribution network, they will be allowed to recoup their investment (Estache and Wren-Lewis 2009). A government that cannot commit to sticking to its original contract—that is, it will not renegotiate a contract as soon as the private investment in infrastructure is made—will not find any private firms willing to invest in infrastructure, leading to an infrastructure deficit.

Buzzacchi and Turati (2014) find that in a situation in which a beneficiary is able to make investments in risk reduction and a benefactor is unable to observe these investments, a decision by the benefactor to cap its total budget for discretionary relief—a commitment device—can improve welfare by reducing the incentive for the beneficiary to underinvest in risk reduction.

The economics of insurance fraud, or misreporting of information, offers some insight into insurance contracting. Townsend (1979) considers a model in which verifying claims is costly, and Lacker and Weinberg (1989) consider an alternative formulation in which verifying claims carries no cost, but the beneficiary is able to falsify claims at some cost. Both models find deductibles to be part of the optimal solution—for losses below a threshold there will be no insurance claim payment—and Lacker and Weinberg's model recognizes the use of underinsurance for extreme, falsifiable perils. Both findings are observed in insurance markets.

The idea of an indexed approach to financial protection probably began with the book by Chakravarti (1920) outlining a detailed proposal for the sale of rainfall-indexed insurance across India. Since then, the idea has gained momentum, particularly for agricultural insurance in developing countries—the traditional farm-based loss adjustment was too expensive and exposed the insurer to moral hazard (Hazell 1992; Skees et al. 1999; Hess et al. 2005)—and for quick post-disaster liquidity at the sovereign level (Ghesquiere and Mahul 2007), where a detailed assessment of losses is too slow for immediate post-disaster needs.

The downside of indexed protection is that the index may not accurately capture the actual situation on the ground, thereby underestimating a severe loss or overestimating a minor one. Unsurprisingly, the more inaccurate the index, the less useful it is as a risk management tool (Clarke 2016) and the lower the demand for indexed protection (Mobarak and Rosenzweig 2012). One might reasonably believe that an inaccurate index would be little used and therefore would do no damage. However, Morsink (2015) found that Ethiopian farmers who were offered indexed protection but did not take it up received significantly lower discretionary post-disaster transfers from other farmers in their community than farmers who were not offered the indexed protection. Low quality indexed protection, it seems, can crowd out informal risk sharing.

How challenging is it to develop accurate indexes, particularly parametric indexes? Jensen et al. (2014) found the accuracy of a parametric index designed by a top academic team to capture the drought-induced mortality of livestock in northern Kenya quite poor. Clarke et al. (2012) conducted a similar but somewhat crude analysis of weather index insurance for Indian farmers. They found that the indexes miss an average of one of every three catastrophe years. Various authors have argued for long-term public investments in accurate indexes (Verdin et al. 2005; Carter et al. 2007; Chantarat et al. 2007; 2009).

Indexed social protection has been implemented by the government of Mexico through its CADENA programme, which provides farmers with free state-level insurance against drought. It has been shown to induce positive risk-management responses demonstrated by the higher yields observed where coverage is available (Fuchs and Wolff 2011). A range of authors have considered the opportunities for and practical challenges of using indexes to trigger shock-responsive social protection (Alderman and Haque 2007; Barnett et al. 2008; Bastagli and Hardman 2015). Pelham et al. (2011) make the case for the importance of shock-responsive social safety nets as a tool for managing disaster risks. In particular, the authors show that safety nets can be useful both pre-disaster, to prevent and mitigate disaster risks, and post-disaster, to cope with the effects of natural disaster shocks. Hobson and Campbell (2012) have investigated the conditions needed to achieve a successful response to shocks through a social safety net.

Building on Hobson and Campbell (2012), Slater and Bhuvanendra (2014) argue that a successful shock response through a safety net programme requires a wide range of institutional and financial arrangements to be in place. Bastagli and Holmes (2014) analyse the criteria necessary to determine whether social protection is effective in responding to shocks, while Grosh et al. (2011) look into what can be learned from previous crises about what may constitute an appropriate crisis response.

5

FINANCE AS THE GLUE

In the early morning of 19 September 1985, an earthquake that registered 8.0 on the Richter scale struck Mexico City, bringing down tens of thousands of buildings and seriously damaging tens of thousands more. It killed at least 5,000 people, and left some 250,000 homeless. The city suffered major damage because of the large magnitude of the quake and the ancient lake bed on which Mexico City sits.

That Mexico should be hit by such an extreme event like this earthquake should not have come as a surprise. With its diverse geography, the country is in fact exposed to a wide variety of geological and hydro-meteorological hazards: earthquakes, volcanoes, tsunamis, hurricanes, wildfires, floods, landslides, and droughts. However, despite being a reasonably well-off middle-income country, it was underprepared to deal with such a calamity, and serious political fallout followed.[1]

The 1985 quake triggered a national dialogue on disaster risk management, and the government of Mexico responded by making it a national priority and by investing to make the country more resilient. One component of this effort was the establishment in 1996 of the Natural Disaster Fund (Fondo Nacional de Desastres Naturales), commonly known as FONDEN. Initially, it was intended to finance post-disaster reconstruction of public infrastructure and low-income housing without the need to gouge other parts of the national budget in the event of a disaster.[2]

Instead of purchasing insurance for each government-owned road, school, hospital, water distribution pipe, electricity line, and piece of other infrastructure, FONDEN acts like an insurer. It covers the full cost of the reconstruction of any federally owned infrastructure and 50 per cent of the cost of any state or municipally owned infrastructure. It finances 'build back better', allowing the reconstruction of more resilient infrastructure at higher standards and the relocation of public buildings and low-income communities to safer zones. To pay for all this, FONDEN has an annual budget allocation from the federal government, akin to an insurer's capital base, and purchases a large reinsurance policy and a catastrophe bond to protect its balance sheet against really big disasters, again like an insurer would.[3]

FONDEN has very clear rules about what reconstruction it will finance and when, similar to the rules that might be found in an insurance policy, but it faces the risk that state governments will inflate their reported losses from disasters and use political pressure to get their way. To protect against this, the government of Mexico has invested in an army of independent loss adjusters who are responsible for objective post-disaster damage assessments and who are overseen jointly by government and its consortium of reinsurers. Reinsurance therefore has a dual purpose: to help pay for reconstruction costs in the worst years and to act as an Odyssean pact, enabling the government of Mexico to credibly commit to objective independent loss adjustment in line with its rules of operation and in turn to insulate FONDEN from potential post-disaster political pressures.[4]

If done well, as in Mexico, financial planning for disasters can be the glue that holds together all the pieces of a carefully defined recovery plan and makes it credible and strong enough to withstand the whirlwind of highly charged post-disaster politics. As the government of Mexico found when developing FONDEN, financial wizardry is important, but it should be the servant, not the master, of a disaster response and recovery plan.

Just as different types of glue are available for fixing different materials, so too different kinds of budgetary and financial instruments are available to governments, donors or other organizations for different kinds of response and recovery plan. Showing the potential use and misuse of these instruments is the purpose of this chapter.

Can Financial Instruments Replace a Disaster Plan?

The amount or type of glue used, or the number or complexity of instruments adopted, is not a good measure of financial planning. Crowing over a big budget for disaster response or preparedness may be misleading. The total budget for disaster response is hardly a measure of effective planning because it can be easily spent poorly. Likewise, it is easy to be seduced by an especially dramatic-sounding financial instrument that promises to solve all problems. Focusing on a particular financial instrument misses the point, and thinking that financial instruments can replace having a plan is misguided. Just because catastrophe reinsurance has been bought or a large contingency fund has been set up does not mean it is the right solution for the circumstances and the organization involved.

Financial instruments will be useful to governments and donors, just as they are to insurers, but for them to give the biggest bang for buck they should form part of the plan, not define the plan. Without something to stick together, playing with glue just makes a mess, and without a clear plan to stick together, whizzy financial instruments are a waste of money. Just as with glue, the usefulness of a financial instrument for financing the risks associated with disasters comes from applying it appropriately.

So, suppose that a government or donor has a plan it wishes to finance. How should it actually develop strategies to bind the plan together and make it credible? Essentially, such an effort has two parts. The first is ensuring that the right amount of money is available quickly when—and only when—it is required by the plan. The second is ensuring that the money is spent on what it is supposed to be spent on and accounted for in a clear, transparent fashion. For example, a ministry of transportation might ensure that US$10 million is available within a week of an earthquake of magnitude 6.0 and that this money actually finances the emergency livelihood support and reconstruction of the lifeline infrastructure for which it is intended. This practice, termed *disaster risk finance,* should bind the various partners to the pre-agreed objectives, decision processes, and implementation modalities. It should give all parties confidence that the plan is credible.

Thinking Like an Insurance Company

In many ways, financial planning for disasters is easier now than ever before because of the huge growth in the range of instruments available and the wealth of knowledge in the insurance industry. There is magic in a good insurance policy: *it creates certainty when an unexpected event occurs.* That means that even though people face lots of risks, the consequences of some of these risks becoming reality are known with certainty. If a kitchen floods but a good home insurance policy is in effect, the result will be lots of inconvenience, but a predetermined share of the material losses will be covered with certainty. If a driver crashes into someone else's car, the insurance company of the car owner, the damaged party, will settle with the driver's insurance company to ensure that the car owner is paid for the damage. The key is certainty, which is created by the credibility of the arrangement: a contract with the insurance company, as well as good regulation and legal frameworks, ensures that insurance companies will indeed do what is expected of them in line with the contract.

Suppose there is an agency in charge of disaster response and preparedness. If it were to learn to think like a reputable insurance company, it would get better at credible financial planning for disasters. Suppose the agency and political leaders have agreed who and what will be protected, against what, and how the protection will work. This 'how' provides the blueprint for a well-defined response and recovery plan to which the agency is committed, as if there is a political contract with the citizens it is entrusted to protect. As discussed in Chapter 3, this agency would then work with engineers and logistical experts to ensure it has a clear idea of how much cash the plan would require in the aftermath of different disasters. It would also work with scientists and risk modellers to understand the likelihood of different types of disaster occurring. These two tracks of technical work would allow the agency to develop a probabilistic assessment of its potential financial liability, its *contingent liability*. Armed with this, the agency would then use actuaries and other financial experts to piece together different budgetary and financial instruments to form a strategy that would ensure it could meet this contingent liability as cost-effectively as possible.

Our advice to such an agency, or to a ministry, or a local or international non-governmental organization (NGO) involved in disaster response is this: think like insurance companies and responses will be more cost-effective with better outcomes. National governments, donors and international organizations would function a lot better if they worked together pre-disaster to clarify what contingent liabilities they would each take on, and then ensured that these liabilities were financed in the most cost-effective way. It does not help anyone to declare that all needs will be met, without a precise, measurable definition of need, a clear plan for how to address the need in a timely manner, and a credible financing strategy. In other words, like an insurer, develop a rules-based plan and then finance the plan, do not try to finance the need directly. As we discussed in Chapter 4, there will always be the need for a back-up for when plans fail or the unforeseen happens, but for the bulk of disaster response and reconstruction there is an urgent need for a clearer articulation of who owns what risk and a credible financing strategy to increase its effectiveness and the value for money it can offer. And this is where thinking like an insurer can really pay off.[5]

Preparing Like an Insurance Company

The contingent liability of a disaster response and recovery plan will encompass the full costs of the risks taken on by the government or agency that owns the plan. This financial liability will include the value of the transfers in cash or in kind that need to reach particular people, the staffing and other logistics costs, the costs of repairing infrastructure, and any other people, firms, organizations, or assets whose losses the plan aims to cover. So how do planners go about designing the financing strategy to cover this entire contingent liability?

The insurance industry has plenty of experience in how to finance a contingent liability. Although medieval begging bowls may still rule disaster finance in many countries, the relevant insurance methods and practices have evolved during centuries of experimenting with risk financing. In fact, insurance companies, pension funds, and their regulators have long solved the key problems of effective disaster risk financing. It is worth explaining how this works.

In a well-regulated market, insurance companies are not allowed to sell insurance policies against disasters unless they can demonstrate up front that they would be able to pay claims as they fall due with a very high degree of certainty. In insurance terms, insurers need to be able to demonstrate that they are actuarially sound, which means that a certified actuary has deemed their financing plan sufficient to meet the needs of the plan, even after an unusually devastating disaster.

To meet this requirement, an insurer traditionally has had a capital base (such as a bank account with money in) to cover all but the most extreme potential losses and it has taken out a reinsurance policy in case it faces such extreme losses that they might exhaust its capital base. The capital base enables the insurer to retain some of the risk, making a profit most of the time but suffering a big loss if claims are much higher than expected. The reinsurance policy enables the insurer to transfer some of the risk to a reinsurer, so that the reinsurer would share in some of the profit if claims are lower than expected but contribute to the cost of very large claims. By buying reinsurance, an insurer transfers part of its balance-sheet risk to the reinsurer, which can retain most of it by holding a massive capital base designed to soak up a diversified portfolio of global risks. In short, the insurance company engages in risk retention via a capital base and in risk transfer via reinsurance. The reinsurance company does the same, although it typically retains more of the risk. Over time, there has been a lot of growth in the variety and type of risk-retention and risk-transfer instruments available to insurers, but the basic principles remain.

These principles should form the basis of a financial strategy for a government or an organization committed to covering particular contingent liabilities. It must decide how much risk it will retain and how much risk it will transfer, and which financial and budgetary instruments to use for this. The same applies to international organizations or donors: they may not see themselves as insurance companies, but could see themselves as reinsurance providers, reinsuring quite extreme risks from countries or organizations, or as insurance brokers, setting up schemes and instruments that allow risk transfer into bigger and better reserve funds and global insurance markets. A combination of risk-retention and risk-transfer instruments can form the basis of a credible financing strategy of response and recovery plans for natural disasters or pandemics, and indeed the various layers of the global humanitarian system.

But before turning to these instruments we would like to recognize another option: a government or organization may not want to prepare or act like an insurance company. Instead, it might prefer to pass on its contingent liability entirely to a regulated insurance company by fully or partially buying insurance policies itself for all the people or specific assets insured. It then prefers to 'buy insurance' rather than to 'be the insurer'. In countries with weak insurance regulation, this may require investment to ensure that commercial insurers manage this disaster risk in an actuarially sound way, or in some cases a government may wish to set up a new insurance provider that is subject to stricter rules. This may be a fruitful route for specific large, publicly owned assets—for example, government buildings in Peru are all legally covered via specific building insurance. And, as will be discussed in more detail shortly, partially subsidizing insurance policies for farmers, homeowners, and firms may be a sensible part of a government strategy, but it can by no means be all.

Choosing among Financial Instruments

What sorts of financial instrument are available to a government or organization to cover the contingent liabilities it has taken on? The budgetary and financial instruments available to a government, its partners, and its insurers to finance the cost of disasters can be categorized across two dimensions: risk retention versus risk transfer and ex ante versus ex post. Table 5.1 describes the key instruments and offers some definitions.[6]

Risk-retention instruments do not take risk off the balance sheet— the cost of a disaster must still be repaid. The instrument just offers more flexibility in how and when one would have to pay. Contingency funds, budget allocations, and lines of contingent credit are all risk-retention instruments, as are budget reallocations, tax increases, and post-disaster credit. By comparison, risk-transfer instruments remove volatility from one's own balance sheet and transfer it to somebody else's. Insurance is the classic risk-transfer instrument, but for governments and insurers the range of risk-transfer instruments is enormous and growing by the day, including indemnity reinsurance, indexed reinsurance, catastrophe bonds, and catastrophe swaps. Soliciting contributions from the international community is a form of risk transfer for governments, although it is typically undisciplined, unpredictable, and slow.

Ex post instruments do not require advance planning. For example, governments could choose to finance a disaster through donor contributions, a budget reallocation, new loans, or tax increases. None of these requires pre-disaster planning. By comparison, ex ante instruments require proactive advance planning and include reserves or contingency funds, budget contingencies, contingent debt facilities, and a range of insurance or other risk-transfer products.

For a government choosing to be the insurer, different instruments have various advantages and disadvantages for credible financing of

Table 5.1: Instruments for Financing Disaster Risk

	Ex ante (arranged before a disaster)	Ex post (arranged after a disaster)
Risk retention	Contingency fund or budget allocation[a]	Budget reallocation
(changing how or when one pays)	Line of contingent credit[b]	Tax increase Post-disaster credit
Risk transfer	Traditional insurance or reinsurance[c]	Discretionary post-disaster aid (begging bowl)
(removing risk from the balance sheet)	Indexed insurance, reinsurance, or derivatives[d] Capital market instruments[e]	

[a] A pre-funded pot of money that can be used for specific purposes, such as responding to a large natural event. Resembles a current account in a bank.

[b] A pre-agreed loan that can only be drawn down in specific pre-agreed circumstances, such as the onset of a large natural event or a declaration of national emergency by government. Slightly resembles an overdraft facility, but one with rules for when the loan can be drawn down.

[c] A contract whereby the insurer or reinsurer is paid a premium and the rules for claim payments are based on the losses incurred, as measured by independent loss adjustors.

[d] A contract whereby the rules for the net transfer to the insurer, reinsurer, or counterparty are based on the index. For insurance and reinsurance, payment of the premium is followed by indexed claim payments. For an indexed derivative, the timing of payments may differ.

[e] Capital market instruments such as catastrophe bonds and catastrophe swaps are financial contracts that can be structured to act in the same way as insurance, but investors, not necessarily reinsurers, provide the protection. A catastrophe bond is an insurance-linked security in which payment of interest and/or principal is suspended or cancelled in the event of a specified catastrophe, such as an earthquake. A catastrophe swap is a contract used by investors to exchange (swap) a fixed payment for a certain portion of the difference between insurance premiums and claims.

well-defined plans. Ex post instruments are not particularly useful for credible pre-disaster plans because typically they cannot be relied on in a contractual sense. Contributions from the international community are famously unreliable: between 2010 and 2014 the annual funding received through UN-coordinated appeals ranged from a low of 29 per cent in 2010, as donors committed large volumes of funds to the response to the Haiti earthquake early in the year, to a high of 57 per cent in 2013.[7] Budget reallocations, borrowing, and new taxes are all certainly possible post-disaster. In practice, however, they all typically give politicians or leaders some degree of discretionary power to write new plans to be financed, or at the very least to rewrite any pre-agreed plan. As argued in Chapter 4, opening the door to such discretion slows everything down and defeats the point of having a well-defined, credible plan. Within such a plan, discretion should be applied only at the technical level, not the policy level. Post-disaster instruments can be useful for financing costs beyond the plan, but not for financing the plan itself.

This is relevant not just for governments funding their own response and recovery plans, but also for humanitarian NGOs, donors, and international organizations committed to providing people and countries with support. They can take responsibility for parts of these plans, or essentially provide reinsurance to local organizations, agencies, and countries for their plans, or broker or fund the emergence of specific risk-transfer instruments that offer governments and organizations new options for financing risk in cost-effective ways. To be able to act in a credible way, as an insurer or a reinsurer, all these organizations will need to decide whether to retain or to transfer these risks. For most, ex post instruments are largely unhelpful: they are hardly going to be able to tax or raise new budgets, and begging bowls and appeals are unreliable. Building up a portfolio of ex ante instruments will be essential to fulfil these organizations' contingent liabilities.

The Challenges and Opportunities of Ex Ante Instruments

Choosing an ex ante financial strategy is not easy, but choices can be informed by technical analysis.

Anyone choosing among ex ante instruments should consider four key dimensions: the discipline required to use an instrument, its cost, its accuracy, and the speed by which it can be converted into cash for spending on a disaster response. For *discipline*, any government or donor with a large reserve fund, budget allocation, or line of credit set aside for financing a specific plan when required will always come under pressure to spend those resources on other things. If a disaster does not happen, governments, international donors, and development banks may all come under criticism for not disbursing funds that have been provided to support development, and the liquidity that has been arranged to finance a specific plan may be re-routed to discretionary spending. When a disaster does strike, even if a financial strategy is successful at providing the right amount of money at the right time, poor public financial management—that is, making sure the money goes where it is supposed to according to the pre-agreed rules—can stymie the entire endeavour. Ex ante risk transfer instruments that transfer contingent liabilities to the market or other agencies make it harder to game the system for political reasons. They will be triggered only in particular circumstances and are more easily directed to the plans they were meant to finance. Plus, they require less discipline by the user because discipline is built into the rules of the contract and is part of the service provided.

In addition to instilling discipline in claim payments, indemnity-based insurance and reinsurance can also instil discipline in risk-reduction investments. Often the actual risk-transfer contract will have a sensible set of conditions for investments in risk reduction and resilience, which will be checked by the insurer or reinsurer. Moreover, any additional investments in risk reduction over and above this should reduce the premium, providing an immediate financial reason for cost-effective risk-reduction investments.[8] The proof of all this? It is no coincidence that Cyclone Patricia, the strongest cyclone ever to make landfall on the Pacific coast, did not cause loss of life when it hit Mexico in October 2015. The entire financing system in Mexico promotes clear risk ownership and appropriate investments in risk reduction and preparedness.

The second issue of importance when choosing among ex ante financial instruments is the *cost*. There are no hard and fast rules for what combination of instruments will be most cost-effective for governments or donors. Relying on principles or rules of thumb for designing a financial strategy is dangerous because the value for money depends so much on the details. Contingency funds can yield low investment returns and be used as a political slush fund, or they can be run in a disciplined manner. Risk-transfer products can be expensive, slow, and unreliable—or they can be cheap, quick, and reliable. Lines of contingent credit can be expensive and discretionary, or cheap and arranged in a way that promotes discipline. Financial expertise is too important to be on the periphery of planning, and, as with any financial product, the risk of being sold a product that is not fit for its purpose is huge. Not for nothing did we argue in Chapter 3 that the men and women of finance must be a core part of the team that develops the plans and then guides the financial strategy through to implementation.

Having said this, there is one rule of thumb that is useful to bear in mind when choosing between risk transfer and risk retention: use risk retention for more frequent losses and risk transfer for the less frequent, larger losses. Typically, a cost-effective financial strategy will use a number of complementary instruments, not unlike ancient cities, which had different layers of defensive walls—the lower, thinner, outermost walls offered cheap but reasonable protection for minor attacks, and the taller, thicker, innermost walls served as a reliable last line of defence for protection against more sizeable, sophisticated, or determined aggressors. Similarly, cost-effective financial strategies for disaster risk financing typically involve risk-retention instruments for smaller, more frequent disasters and risk-transfer instruments for larger, more extreme disasters. This arrangement appears over and over in risk finance, from insurers and reinsurers to mutual insurance societies and the insurance captives[9] of large multinational companies.

This principle is relevant for risk financing by governments, even if they usually can handle large losses on their budget.[10] The reason is the cost of liquidity. When a government chooses to retain disaster risk, it effectively needs to have a large pot of money sitting somewhere, waiting for a potential disaster. That pot might take the form of a contingency fund or a budget allocation, or the government may pay a lender to keep a pot of money available that it can borrow from quickly in the event of a disaster, essentially an overdraft facility. Either way, the government is paying the full cost of the liquidity itself. But this will not be attractive for less frequent losses: the cash held would be rarely used and thus costly. Risk transfer is, then, more attractive because it allows the cost of liquidity be shared with others: a regular payment can be made to have access to substantial liquid means when required.

The final two key issues to consider when choosing among financial instruments are *accuracy* and *speed*. Here the intuition is straightforward: wherever possible, the timing and triggers of the financial instruments—in particular the triggers for any line of contingent credit and risk-transfer instruments—should match precisely the triggers in the plan. If the triggers in the plan are parametric, then parametric triggers should be applied to the risk transfer. If the triggers are based on individual loss adjustment, the risk transfer should be based on this loss adjustment. Finally, speed matters, and it must play a central role in deciding among instruments. If the plan requires immediate access to financial resources, then instruments need to be chosen that offer this. In general, if it is difficult to access risk-transfer or even risk-retention instruments that match the rules in the plan in terms of accuracy or speed, it is likely that the rules of the plan are unworkable in a practical sense, and they may need to be rethought.

Acting Like an Insurance Company

Governments, agencies, or organizations that have prepared themselves like an insurance company for the contingent liabilities they have decided to take on can go a step further: they can start acting like an insurance company, offering a contractual relationship to clients that guarantees support when natural disasters hit. They can learn from modern insurance market practice about how to behave like an insurer and then emulate an insurer, sometimes at lower cost.

Programmes in Mexico and Kenya have done just that with good results.[11] As we described in Chapter 1 and elsewhere, in Mexico FONDEN is liable for the cost of reconstructing public infrastructure and low-income housing after natural disasters, and it operates akin to insurance, with clear rules on what it will pay for, a financial strategy that combines a contingency fund with risk-transfer instruments, independent loss adjustment, and strong incentives for risk reduction and resilience.

Also as described earlier, in Kenya about 400,000 pastoralist households are registered in the Hunger Safety Net Programme, and the 100,000 of those deemed to be the most in need receive regular cash transfers. In times of drought, however, the programme temporarily scales up by making quick cash transfers to some or all of the remaining 300,000 pastoralist households, providing them with the means to protect their families and their animals. These additional pastoralists are in effect covered by an insurance policy—a social safety net that pays a cash transfer to a predefined group of pastoralists when the rains fail, without delay and without questions, so they can afford to buy food and fodder even though the harvest is bad. Above and beyond what is being given to them for free, they also are given the option of buying affordable insurance for more peace of mind. The programme has simple parametric triggers for payments, in this case satellite data on the 'greenness' of ground vegetation, which is a good proxy for drought-related stress in these areas. The government contributes a regular budget for normal years, and an international donor, the United Kingdom's Department for International Development, acts like a reinsurer, providing additional funds as needed to cover the pre-agreed rules for scaling up in extreme years.

Although Ethiopia's Productive Safety Net Programme covers millions of people and has positive impacts on people's lives and livelihoods (see Chapter 1),[12] it does not operate with defined triggers.

However, since its inception in 2005 it has had a facility to scale up the provision of payments to additional beneficiaries and include new beneficiaries in response to droughts. To secure its funding, a risk-financing mechanism was introduced in 2009 to allow the rapid mobilization of additional resources in the event of an emergency. For example, in 2011 the mechanism was triggered, providing support to an additional 3.1 million beneficiaries for three months and extending the duration of transfers for 6.5 million existing beneficiaries for the same length of time. It now serves as the backbone of current responses to drought because it covers some of the most vulnerable in the population. However, further improvements could be made: it lacks early and defined triggers that may cause delays, and there is no a priori registration of those who may be covered when droughts or other extreme events take place.

Some governments may recognize the virtue of insurance-like schemes, but they are reluctant to be the insurer themselves. A few countries such as Panama, Peru, and Colombia legally require all government buildings to be insured.[13] Where farmers, homeowners, and businesses may be able to bear some of these risks themselves, many governments do not want to take on the full contingent liabilities for losses to assets and livelihoods in the event of a disaster. Governments may provide incentives or subsidies for people to buy insurance, either using existing commercial insurance companies or at times setting up national insurance companies to implement these schemes. For example, the governments of France, Japan, New Zealand, Spain, Turkey, the state of California, and the Republic of China (Taiwan), have all set up institutions that offer property catastrophe insurance to homeowners and businesses, and the governments of Canada, Cyprus, Greece, India, the Islamic Republic of Iran, and the Philippines have all established government-owned insurers to provide agricultural insurance.[14] These schemes, and schemes in which government partners with private insurers, typically offer subsidized insurance whereby government contributes towards the cost of insurance. In some countries, these schemes are perceived to have offered a reasonable balance, restricting the contingent liability of the government to make a sensible plan feasible, by expecting individuals to take some responsibility by paying part of the cost of financial protection against disasters themselves.

Although it is often successful, this approach of governments supporting disaster insurance markets has not always been so. Sometimes, these schemes are not run on an actuarially sound basis and end up having to be bailed out by the government after a disaster.[15] Even when such schemes are actually sound, a government often succumbs to temptation to structure its subsidies to undermine the fundamental principle of risk-based pricing, whereby the premium reflects the underlying risk—for example, by capping the premium paid by the policyholder. Such approaches may be attractive politically, because subsidies target those at highest risk, but by structuring subsidies in this way governments encourage people to take on more risk, or at the very least to underinvest in sound risk management, because by doing so the value of the subsidy is kept as high as possible.[16] Making insurance compulsory is often regarded as a useful strategy for increasing the number of people protected, thereby reducing the potential for the presentation of begging bowls post-disaster. However, such an approach places a very high burden of care on government to ensure that products offer value, because consumers typically have no power to hold insurance companies to account.

Efforts by governments and donors to develop unsubsidized markets for disaster insurance have not generally been too successful, particularly in poorer countries.[17] Over the last decade, international donors have supported over a hundred pilot programmes aimed at providing unsubsidized weather-index insurance markets to protect poor, vulnerable farmers against the vagaries of the weather. A typical goal of these programmes is for farmers to pay the full cost of their financial protection against shocks, so that after a large disaster they reliably receive fast cash and have no need to call on government or other benefactors for help. The policies are parametric: payments are triggered when low rainfall or another easily measured indicator is reached.

Although noble in their intentions, only a few of these programmes have survived beyond the donor support, and for those that have, there are unanswered questions about how good the protection would actually be in a disaster. Many poor farmers seem unwilling to pay the full cost of their financial protection themselves, and so most agricultural insurance programmes for poor farmers that are still in force are subsidized. No doubt, there is room to continue to experiment with such schemes, because they could offer some certainty, not least when governments or agencies fail to act as insurers instead. But they are probably not quite ready to be a means of protecting large vulnerable populations during disasters. For that, governments and other benefactors will continue to play a role, and are likely to have to retain these contingent liabilities, acting as insurers themselves by covering either fully or partially the costs of providing financial protection.

The Building Blocks of a Better System

The virtues of moving towards ex ante financing of disaster risk cannot be emphasized enough. Away goes the primacy of the begging-bowl financing model, leaving space for the emergence of a system that focuses on well-defined, credible plans, with better decision making and clarity. The programmes under way in Kenya, Ethiopia, and Mexico, while different, demonstrate how good pre-disaster planning and preparation by governments can help all those affected by a natural disaster get back on their feet as quickly as possible.

However, governments cannot typically afford to protect everyone fully against every possible disaster. Similarly, if government leaves it to insurance companies to try to persuade people to pay the full cost of insurance against disasters themselves, experience suggests that very few will end up being protected. But there is good experience with governments joining in partnership with private insurers to offer subsidized insurance for agriculture or for property to cope with natural disasters. Subsidies tend to cover things such as investments in data, awareness, and education, and often part of the insurance premium as well, and offer a way for government to offer to pay its share if vulnerable people are willing to pay their share as well. For governments that would otherwise be called on to play the role of benefactor after a disaster, subsidized insurance solutions can offer a planned alternative that provides better incentives and faster support.

Other instruments are also available and have been used by various countries. In recent years, countries or organizations acting on behalf of them have bought insurance products on the international market. For example, in 2006 the World Food Programme bought a parametric policy for Ethiopia from AXA that would have paid out US$7 million in case of drought, but it was not renewed. Likewise, beginning in 2008, Malawi experimented with the use of a parametric drought insurance policy, but discontinued that experiment after several years. In other examples, Mexico has been buying catastrophe bonds linked to FONDEN for some years, and the Caribbean Catastrophe Risk Insurance Facility recently purchased one as well.

Development banks and other organizations have also been devising promising instruments. Targeting middle-income countries, the World Bank has developed a Deferred Drawdown Option for Catastrophe Risks (Cat DDO). This loan can be triggered when a natural disaster occurs. It offers immediate post-disaster liquidity, conditional upon having a sound disaster risk management programme in place. Ten countries have made use of this instrument.[18]

Groups of countries, with donor support and assistance from international organizations, have also set up specialized institutions targeting disaster risk management. The Caribbean Catastrophe Risk Insurance Facility (CCRIF), established by the Caribbean Community in 2007 with support from the World Bank and a range of donors, sells parametric earthquake and tropical cyclone coverage, and more recently excess rainfall coverage. Products pay within fourteen days of an event and are designed to offer quick liquidity to governments for emergency response and reconstruction. For the 2015–16 season, it sold insurance to sixteen Caribbean island states and one Central

American country, all but two of whom pay the full premium themselves.[19] The Pacific Catastrophe Risk Assessment and Financing Initiative (PCRAFI), a partnership between the Pacific Community, development banks, donors, and scientists, has provided five Pacific island states with subsidized insurance against earthquakes and tropical cyclones since 2013.[20] The African Risk Capacity, set up as a specialized agency of the African Union, provides rainfall-based parametric drought insurance, initially to four African countries in 2014.[21] And, after Ebola, it is likely that some countries and international organizations will establish an insurance facility for pandemic risks, providing insurance based on the incidence of particular highly infectious diseases in developing countries that could pose risks for pandemics.

And there will always be a need for back-up in foreseen circumstances, or when even the most carefully designed plan fails. For such cases, ex post instruments may be necessary, and here too the details matter. Budget reallocations may involve taking money from projects with a high social benefit, thereby making the opportunity cost of funds quite high. Or, at the other extreme, the opportunity costs of funds could be very low, such as in the aftermath of the 2015 Nepal earthquake. Discussions with the government suggest that the emergency procurement processes actually enabled it to invest budget funds that were not disbursed.

Post-disaster fund-raising can also be implemented better or worse, depending on how contributors arrange their finances. Arranging funding beforehand (instead of resorting to unpredictable appeals) will pay here as well in terms of speed and effectiveness. For example, over the last decade the United Nations Central Emergency Response Fund has operated as a contingency fund that can spend relatively quickly in response to appeals to the humanitarian system, targeting underfunded humanitarian crises. Its annual budget is typically US$400 million. This has been an important innovation in the move towards pre-disaster funding, even though the fund is relatively small compared with the total annual humanitarian funding of approximately US$10 billion. This sort of approach to funding global appeals could be developed further by, for example, expanding the size or moving further towards an objective, transparent, rules-based approach based on monitoring both natural disasters and the effectiveness of national responses.[22]

NGOs will also continue to play their role as back-up. And here we also see helpful innovation, moving away from post-disaster begging bowls, fragmentation, and benefactor behaviours. For example, the Start Fund is a pooled funding mechanism managed by nineteen UK-based NGOs providing relatively small-scale funding to NGOs for underfunded emergencies. It is supported by Irish Aid and the UK Department for International Development.[23] Its explicit purpose is to ensure fast disbursement based on collective decision making.

These market and non-market based instruments will not guarantee better responses to disasters. Finance or bigger budgets are not in themselves the key problem to be resolved. But the existence and growth of this plethora of pre-disaster instruments for risk transfer do present the possibility of achieving credibly pre-financed, well-defined plans in a more cost-effective and reliable way. And that may then also reduce the need for a large back-up system for natural disasters based on post-disaster fund-raising and other begging bowls. It would also create the space for the humanitarian system to focus its efforts and fund-raising more on the less tractable humanitarian challenges, such as those in conflict settings.

Recapping...

1. Financial and budgetary instruments are the glue that holds credible plans together and makes them strong enough to withstand the whirlwind of highly charged post-disaster politics.
2. When designing and implementing disaster risk financing strategies, details matter. Financial experts add value. It is important to pay for financial advice and build in-house expertise.

3. Discipline, cost, accuracy, and speed all matter when structuring a disaster risk financing strategy. Speed matters but not all resources are needed at once.
4. The triggers in the financial strategy should match the triggers in the plan. Traditional reinsurance can be particularly useful for locking in plans for reconstruction, and indexed reinsurance can play the same role for financing indexed early actions.
5. Partially subsidized financial instruments can be used to encourage others to contribute towards the cost of well-defined plans.

A Snapshot of the Literature

The economics literature focuses on two rationales for governments transferring disaster-associated risk to regulated insurers, reinsurers, or capital markets. The first rationale is that, by swapping uncertain contingent liabilities for a more predictable premium or fee, risk transfer can reduce a government's *budget volatility*. This rationale draws on early theoretical work on the use of financial markets to intermediate risk sharing by Debreu (1954), Borch (1962), and Arrow (1971). Although Arrow and Lind (1970) argue that national governments should be able to diversify risk perfectly and therefore should have no need for risk transfer, Ghesquiere and Mahul (2007: 2010) demonstrate that this argument does not hold in two specific cases: where a country is exposed to potential disaster losses that are large relative to the national wealth, and where risk-retention instruments available for immediate post-disaster funding needs are imperfect.

In practice, the former argument does not seem to be very strong, even for the extreme case of vulnerable small island states. Von Peter et al. (2012) use a large panel data set of 203 countries and jurisdictions over fifty-two years to argue that having larger insurance payouts after a disaster helps post-disaster economic recovery, but because they do not consider the cost of insurance they are unable to argue whether, on average, insurance was beneficial to growth. Bevan and Adam

(2015) address this issue by applying a recent macroeconomic model developed by the International Monetary Fund's Research Department (Berg et al. 2012) to Jamaica's tropical cyclone risk. They find that ex post tax-financed reconstruction of public assets would be slightly more cost-effective than insurance, even though it would lead to slower restoration of the public capital stock. Essentially, their finding is that even though Jamaica is a small island state, exposed to large potential shocks, these shocks are not large relative to national income, and smoothing the cost of the shock over time at the national level is slightly more cost-effective than insurance, a finding reminiscent of Gollier (2003). There is empirical support for the argument that risk-retention instruments for immediate post-disaster funding needs are imperfect (World Bank 2014a; 2015). This means that there does seem to be a budget volatility motivation for risk transfer for immediate post-disaster funding needs, but not for the bulk of reconstruction costs, which are not incurred immediately after a disaster.

The second rationale for government to engage in risk transfer is in situations in which the beneficiary pays part of the cost of protection and insurers and reinsurers are better able to implement *risk-based pricing* than government. Under risk-based pricing, investments in risk reduction would lead to lower-cost protection, thereby increasing the attractiveness to the beneficiary of investments in risk reduction with a positive net present value (Picard 2008; Jaffee and Russell 2013; Charpentier and Le Maux 2014; Kunreuther 2015). Governments do seem to find risk-based pricing challenging to implement in the absence of independent public or private institutions empowered to implement it (Cummins and Mahul 2009).

One further argument for risk transfer, so far inadequately researched, is as a *commitment device*—that is, a way in which government can commit itself to data systems and rules for how money will flow after a disaster, protect the system against discretion and fraud, and protect public policy from the dilemma of time inconsistency as discussed in Chapter 4. The use of financial instruments as commitment devices is not new and is, for example, the main explanation for the success of commitment savings products observed across developing countries (Armendáriz and Morduch 2010). In the case of disaster risk financing, this rationale has been argued by practitioners such as the World Bank (2014a) and Phaup and Kirschner (2010), but as yet there has been no empirical analysis of its merits.

Three arguments are commonly made against government engaging with regulated risk-transfer providers for the joint management of disaster risk: (1) the provider may risk insolvency (Charpentier and Le Maux 2014); (2) for catastrophe risk that is difficult to quantify, regulated risk-transfer providers may not be able to offer attractive prices (Carter 2013; Kunreuther 2015); and (3) government may face a lack of competition (von Ungern-Sternberg 2004).

A variety of arguments have also been made for government providing subsidies or making insurance compulsory. Hill et al. (2014) and Carter et al. (2014) argue that subsidies for agricultural insurance can be designed to correct a clearly stated and well-documented market failure or equity concern. This argument builds on a number of careful impact evaluations of index insurance programmes for farmers, which support, in turn, the argument that credible indexed protection can instil good incentives for climate-smart, risk-sensitive investments. For example, Karlan et al. (2012), Mobarak and Rosenzweig (2012), Janzen and Carter (2013), and Elabed and Carter (2014) all find that index insurance significantly boosts investment or reduces asset decumulation. However, demand for insurance from farmers is still quite low in the absence of subsidies (see, for example, Cole et al. 2013) and quite sensitive to recent experience (Cole et al. 2014).

The low penetration of disaster insurance is, however, not restricted to agricultural insurance in developing countries. In the absence of subsidies, Pomeroy (2010) reports that only 12 per cent of homeowners' policies in California include earthquake insurance despite the compulsory offer rule whereby any insurer who sells homeowners' insurance must explicitly give clients the option to include earthquake insurance in their policy. Kunreuther and Pauly (2006) point to the fact that only 40 per cent of the residents of Orleans Parish had flood insurance before Hurricane Katrina slammed into New Orleans in 2005. They propose compulsory but subsidized insurance for homeowners as a policy option, motivating the arguments of Jaffee and Russell (2013).

A wide range of practical experience around the world in designing and implementing credible ex ante financial plans for disasters is documented. A rich literature has emerged in the United States, stimulated by the rapid growth in federal government involvement in financial protection against disasters (see, for example, Kunreuther and Michel-Kerjan 2009) and in developing countries (Gurenko et al. 2006; Cummins and Mahul 2009; World Bank 2014a; 2015). McCulloch et al. (2015) consider the potential application of disaster risk financing solutions by humanitarian actors and microfinance institutions, and Mahul and Stutley (2010) and Carter et al. (2014) provide recent analyses of the conceptual and practical opportunities and challenges for government support of agricultural insurance. Private-sector risk carriers regularly produce research on the global market for disaster risk transfer, some of which is publicly available (see, for example, Swiss Re 2015).

6

MOVING FORWARD . . .

The evidence is still growing, but what is already clear is that a better way of dealing with disasters is possible. Three things are essential: a coordinated plan for post-disaster action agreed in advance; a fast, evidence-based decision-making process; and a funding model, based on risk financing principles, to credibly lock in the plan and rules.

Why Are We Even Talking about This?

Disaster losses are huge, averaging US$250–$300 billion a year, according to the United Nations. The number of deaths, serious injuries, and health issues arising from disasters climbs into the hundreds of thousands each year. Losses are trending up, partly from economic growth and urbanization and partly from climate change—but also because development is often not carried out in a risk-informed way. Cities are built along fault lines; schools are erected without regard to the most basic building codes; roads are constructed in areas where they will be washed away by a minor flood; and houses are built on flood plains.

Earthquakes, droughts, floods, storms, and epidemics are natural events, but the number of deaths or the amount of damage depends on the actions of individuals and governments both before and after those events. When extreme natural events turn into disasters, the response from governments and the international community is often generous. This generosity is driven in part by the feeling that it is right and proper to support disaster victims and in part by the recognition that it makes for good politics. In fact, disaster relief is often a media circus—a time for national leaders to get visibility, particularly in election years—and it makes for good press releases by international donors.

The actual response to a disaster, however, is typically too late, too fragmented, and too unreliable. This is begging-bowl financing at its worst, with farmers, homeowners, and local governments pleading for help from the national government, and the national government making appeals to international donor governments and other bene-factors. What does all this mean? Planning for disaster response does not begin in earnest until after the disaster, and that is too late. Nobody works out who will do what and who will pay for what until the crisis is unfolding, leading to a fragmented, inefficient response. And if media or political attention moves elsewhere, or if national governments or international donors have already spent their annual disaster contin-gency budgets, what help is received may not be enough.

The ambiguity over who will be generous, for what, and how much they will contribute produces poor incentives for planning. Why would a local government take time and care to prepare a serious disaster plan if it is not clear whether it will be funded or implemented by the central government until after the event? Why would a gov-ernment in a poor country set up response mechanisms beforehand if it is unclear whether the funding will arrive to implement those mechanisms, or, even when it does come, whether the benefactor will want to decide what to spend it on? Ambiguity also leads to a system with extremely poor incentives for risk reduction. Why would a municipal government invest in hospitals if the national government could always be persuaded to pay for most of any disaster-related damage? Why would a homeowner buy disaster insurance or invest in a home away from the flood plain if compensation is paid for every flood? Why would farmers invest in better water management if agricultural loans are cancelled whenever there is a minor drought? Why would a government invest in alternative livelihood opportun-ities in drought-prone areas if donors will bail them out when there is a serious drought?

What Is the Solution?

There is nothing wrong with funding for disasters based on generosity. Indeed, it is to be applauded. However, it is much better for generous governments and donors to acknowledge and clarify their generosity *before* any disaster—that is, for benefactors to become leaders. They should be clear about what risk they own and what risk belongs to others.

What does this mean for planning? It means thinking and preparing like an insurance company. It means being upfront about who or what governments and their partners will protect and against what, how much others will have to pay, and what the conditions for protection will be. It means getting the right professionals in the room, working with each other and political leaders to develop a credible plan. It means investing in risk information to inform plans and in risk communication so that everyone understands the potential threat from natural hazards and values the protection being offered. It means investing in fraud-resistant data systems that can trigger automatic post-disaster action, turning early warning into early action. It means building up implementation capabilities so that relief and reconstruction can be implemented like clockwork. And it means working with bureaucrats to provide guidance on the thorny trade-offs over who or what to protect and with financial experts to assemble budgetary and financial instruments that credibly commit them to the plan.

All this is challenging, but it is possible. And it is already starting. Efforts are under way around the world to toss out the begging bowl and turn benefactors into leaders. Learning from the response to the Ebola outbreak and from responding to various recent natural disasters, international organizations and think tanks are changing their approaches to disasters so they can achieve better decision making and preparedness, and they are offering proposals, some consistent with ours. More pre-disaster financing instruments are becoming available.

Nevertheless, most of the innovation is at the national level, where governments have begun to develop well-defined, pre-financed plans that will be implemented in the event of a disaster. These plans are not designed to cover everything that may be needed in the aftermath of a disaster, but they are simple enough for political leaders to communicate to their constituents—even in a sound bite if they must. No vague statements are made that all needing help will be covered. Rather, a credible commitment is made to responding decisively to protect pre-identified people or property in a specific way against specific perils. And countries are locked in using financial instruments, so that in the event of a disaster those instruments can be implemented quickly and decisively without any need for further debate or deliberation from political leaders. Where changes have been carefully evaluated, big improvements in response times and outcomes are evident.

What Are the Challenges?

Four challenges stand out. If governments and their partners do not address each of these attempts to move away from the begging bowl, planning will be futile—just another bureaucratic exercise to gather dust in someone's drawer. It is best, then, to address these four challenges head-on.

Making Difficult Pre-Disaster Trade-offs

Neither national governments nor international donors can afford to protect everyone against every possible disaster. For that reason, the difficult trade-offs should be made before disasters. Trade-offs are not easy, but they are already being made implicitly in the current system. Making explicit trade-offs before a disaster allows proper planning and instils good incentives in the system, but political leaders will need help in developing plans that can be sold to their constituencies.

The foundations of a credible plan could be an existing social safety net with the commitment, financing arrangements, and logistics to expand it to a well-defined broader group when an extreme event of an intensity that would trigger an automatic response takes place. The social safety net could expect certain actions by those who would be part of the expanded coverage, such as registering before the event and perhaps making a financial contribution or taking some actions at the local community level to increase resilience to a crisis. Kenya's Hunger Safety Net Programme is a good example of such a plan.

A credible plan for response and recovery after a storm or earthquake could specify how repairs to public infrastructure will be triggered and prioritized (with the financing plan agreed beforehand) and how for a specified period those who lost homes or livelihoods would be supported. It could also specify that homeowners would be expected to pay part of the cost of disaster insurance, which is conditional on following a basic building code if they want to be eligible for government support to rebuild their houses afterwards. Mexico's National Disaster Fund (FONDEN) offers such a plan for public infrastructure.

Once there is clarity on who is being protected and against what and on who is paying, there may be difficult trade-offs over who will implement what. Again, this is difficult but necessary if the objective is coordinated, not fragmented, implementation.

Providing Protection, Not Relief

There is much political capital to be gained from being a benefactor. In fact, research on evidence-based electoral politics suggests that politicians have far more to win from focusing on disaster relief than on risk reduction and response preparation. But that does not bode well for planners setting out to convince politicians to come on board. So how can planners make their proposals politically attractive?

The trick is to help politicians explain to their constituents that planning is the route to providing protection: investing now, not just offering relief when things go wrong. By communicating the idea of protection, a politician can clarify what risk the government or agency owns and what risk it does not. Disaster relief is attractive politics, and so the professionals must help political leaders ensure that protection becomes good politics, too.

Selling the focus on protection will be easier when the electorate and commerce are well informed about the future disaster risk. If nobody understands disaster risk, a political statement that people are protected will not be politically cost-effective, even if the benefits for people and the economy are overwhelming.

In some countries, better responses over time have become the norm following better preparedness and planning. For example, over many decades Japan has become a success story in which science has infused the public consciousness and led to good planning. The Japanese model offers strong motivation for investing in the communication of disaster risk information at all levels of society so that better, smarter, disaster risk management solutions are politically sellable and sustainable.

Getting Others to Pay Their Share

Governments and international donors should aim for coordinated, pre-financed defined plans, with clear responsibilities for coordinated implementation and a credible joint financing strategy, and not the current myriad of initiatives. Each country could have a small number of well-defined plans for different key risks, or one generic plan that can be adapted for different risks. For some risks, such as pandemics, a plan covering multiple countries may be appropriate. To make this work, all parties will have to be tied to the mast like Odysseus, and that will not be easy (see Chapter 3).

A requirement will be political courage and commitment by the key players involved. Indeed, politicians will have to care—for their people, for the poor—for all this to work. Leadership from a few important benefactors could go a long way towards changing the incentives of everyone else in the system, showcasing how contributing to defined, credible plans could be an attractive strategy for others. Governments and donors should not be shy about offering funding for precise plans conditional on others providing co-financing, or plans in which they publicly announce that they will match contributions from others. Multilateral agencies such as the World Bank are already facilitating such co-financing solutions when they implement shock-responsive social safety nets financed through concessionary lines of credit. In such arrangements, the government pays part of the full economic cost and donors finance the remainder. It is hoped that more examples of this kind of scheme appear, with governments taking clear ownership of such arrangements. This is the trajectory for schemes such as Ethiopia's Productive Safety Net Programme and Kenya's Hunger Safety Net Programme.

Learning by Doing and Having a Backup

The evidence for changing the funding model and moving towards pre-financed, precise, credible plans is overwhelming. However, the evidence on what plans should look like is still emerging. Professionals will have to work together to put sensible, country-specific or problem-specific plans together and will need to learn by doing.

At the same time, dogma cannot replace reason. Rules-based plans sometimes go wrong, and reality sometimes takes even the most careful planners by surprise. For example, a precise plan might be designed for a drought and then there would be a flood.

For unforeseen events, national relief financed by begging bowls and the international humanitarian system, with their post-disaster assessment and principled deliberation, is actually the appropriate system to serve as a catch-all back-up. It is not, however, the best solution for natural hazards for which one can reasonably plan, because it asks for leadership too late, does not lead to a fast, coordinated response, and does not promote good incentives for risk reduction. Arrangements that target pre-disaster protection are better where possible, but arrangements that target post-disaster need are useful as a back-up. And the more the financing of this back-up can be pre-arranged between willing contributors, with clear rules and commitments, the more effective the back-up.

Getting Started: Taking the First Steps

The process begins with generous people owning up to and clarifying their generosity before a disaster. Here are some steps that could offer a starting point.

First, one or more benefactors would lead the shift from begging bowls to well-defined, credible plans and would provide financial and political incentives for others to jointly pay into the plans. These benefactors could be national leaders, embracing precise plans as a way to give them more predictability about post-disaster support from donors and subnational governments and to promote good incentives for people and firms. Or they could be international leaders, as contributors to the humanitarian system, seeking to move away from a system filled with procrastination, appeals, and post-disaster strategic manoeuvring and towards a system in which their political contract with other governments and people is clarified in a way that promotes good incentives to invest in risk reduction. Or it could be a combination of national and international leaders.

Second, national governments would own the development of precise, credible plans as part of an iterative dialogue with risk modellers, communicators, implementers, bureaucrats, and financiers. This process would best be led by government, but in collaboration with others in order to work jointly towards a more efficient, faster, and less costly system to address disaster risks, including response preparedness but also risk reduction. Politicians will need to find ways to clarify to their citizens what the protection offered will entail. They will also have to specify the efforts government, firms, and citizens would be expected to make to ensure that development is more risk-sensitive and resilient.

Third, implementing agencies would change the ways in which they plan. This means actively engaging with others to develop well-defined, credible plans that have political buy-in and are fully financed up front, and then to ensure that there will be the capacity to implement them.

And they should be willing to agree on coordination, decision, and implementation structures beforehand.

Finally, financiers would need to be at the table from the start to help design, cost, and implement disaster risk financing strategies for pre-financing these well-defined plans. They should also help advise on the balance between risk retention and risk transfer in the funding of the plans. Crucially, as explained in Chapter 5, they should help all contributors to the plan move towards pre-disaster financing instruments—that is, from emergency budget reallocations, emergency debt issuance, and begging bowls towards well-managed reserve funds, lines of contingent credit, and the plethora of insurance and reinsurance instruments that are currently available on the market or through regional organizations such as the Caribbean Community, Pacific Community, and African Union.

Dulling Disasters, Now!

This is a good time to prepare better for disasters and sort out their financing. Humanitarian disasters are unacceptable across the world, and, faced with forecasts of a rising number of extreme events, the world should be better prepared to offer reasonable protection at the lowest possible cost. But much work has yet to be done. Globally, nationally, and locally, as governments or as part of the global humanitarian system, benefactors of all stripes would do well to think and act more like insurance and reinsurance companies. Each actor should define better who and what it will protect—and rebuild the system from these contingent liabilities and their gaps.

Today's disasters need leaders and humanitarians who do not just respond emotionally and energetically to crises, but who plan beforehand with clear and strong commitment devices, using political, legal, and financial mechanisms based on specific triggers for action and financing. Learning from research and resisting the song of the Sirens, they can make sure the system works. The new approach may result in less airtime for disasters, appeals, emotions, and adrenaline, and more tutorials on the principles of insurance. By dulling disasters—as in making them less intense—we may make them a little dull and boring as well. But that will be worth it.

Recapping...

1. Discretionary begging-bowl financing does not work well for disasters. It is too slow, leads to a fragmented response, and encourages underinvestment in risk reduction and preparedness.
2. To get around this problem, generous people and their political leaders should own up to and clarify who or what they will protect and against what and how much others will have to pay. They should be willing to think as if they are an insurance company.
3. This means making trade-offs over who or what to protect before disasters. This process is not easy, but it is necessary for a system with good incentives.
4. Leaders should focus on providing protection, not relief, and using financial incentives to encourage others to own up to and finance their share up front.
5. The international humanitarian system is still needed, but it should act as a back-up when plans fail. It should not be the first line of defence for floods, earthquakes, droughts, storms, or pandemics.

GLOSSARY

area average index An index calculated as the area average mean economic loss. It is calculated either as a population mean or as a sample mean. For example, the average crop yield for maize in a subdistrict as measured by a series of statistical samples of crop yield is a type of area yield index.

attribution error A cognitive bias whereby people erroneously attribute their own or someone else's behaviour to a certain cause. In the context of disaster risk management, voters may make attribution errors by attributing investments in preparedness expenditures to future government administrations instead of the government administration that made the investments.

begging-bowl financing A discretionary ex post model for funding losses. In the case of disaster risk, beneficiaries such as individuals, communities, local and national governments, international agencies, and non-governmental organizations would be required to wait until after a disaster to request, negotiate, and secure funding from benefactors.

benefactor An individual or institution that retains discretion until after a disaster over what it will fund, rather than agreeing before a disaster what it will fund.

budget allocation An amount of funding set aside to cover specific planned expenditures. In the context of disaster risk management, a budget allocation can be made so that it can be accessed only in the event of a disaster.

capital base Money contributed by the shareholders who first purchased shares in a company plus retained earnings.

capital market instrument Any financial contract that can be structured to act in the same way as reinsurance, but with investors, not necessarily reinsurers, providing the protection. Examples are catastrophe bonds and catastrophe swaps.

catastrophe bond An insurance-linked security in which payment of interest and/or principal is suspended or cancelled in the event of a specified catastrophe such as an earthquake.

catastrophe swap A contract used by investors to exchange (swap) a fixed payment for a certain portion of the difference between insurance premiums and claims.

contingency fund A reserve fund designated for financing disaster losses. Allocations to the contingency fund can be made through budget allocations of the national or local governments, international agencies, communities, or a combination of these. Funds are made available immediately after a disaster and are disbursed using clear and simple rules.

contingent credit A financial tool that provides governments with immediate access to funds following disaster events to enable a more rapid and efficient response. This type of financing is typically used to finance losses caused by recurrent natural disasters. A line of contingent credit is an ex ante instrument that allows borrowers to prepare for a natural disaster by securing access to financing before a disaster strikes.

contingent liability A potential future expenditure. In the case of disaster risk, a government or organization's contingent liability is a random variable denoting the liability contingent on potential disaster events.

disaster risk finance The financial protection of populations against disaster events. Disaster risk finance strategies increase the ability of national and local governments, homeowners, businesses, agricultural producers, and low-income populations to respond more quickly and resiliently to disasters.

disaster risk management The systematic process of using administrative directives, organizations, and operational skills and capacities to implement strategies, policies, and improved coping capacities in order to lessen the adverse impacts of hazards and the possibility of disaster.

disaster risk reduction The concept and practice of reducing disaster risks through systematic efforts to analyse and manage the causal factors of disasters, including through reduced exposure to hazards, reduced vulnerability of people and property, wise management of land and the environment, and improved preparedness for adverse events.

emergency recovery phase The disaster response phase that follows the emergency relief phase. During recovery, initial relief efforts have been completed; typically people have access to food, water, and temporary shelter, and children are able to attend school. The recovery phase can last several weeks or months, depending on the initial situation of the country.

emergency relief phase The disaster response phase that begins immediately after a disaster. During the emergency relief phase, key objectives include ensuring food security, shelter, and medical care. The duration of the relief phase depends on the initial situation of the country following the disaster event.

ex ante Latin for 'from before'. In the context of disaster events, ex ante instruments are arranged before the event, and ex ante decisions are made at that time as well.

ex post Latin for 'from after'. In the context of disaster events, ex post instruments are arranged after the event, and ex post decisions are made at that time as well.

global humanitarian system The network of interconnected institutional and operational entities through which humanitarian assistance is provided when local and national resources are insufficient to meet the needs of the affected population.

hidden action Within a principal agent problem, the case in which the principal cannot observe the behaviour of the agent. Hidden action is a type of informational asymmetry. See *moral hazard*.

humanitarian aid In general terms, the aid and action designed to save lives, alleviate suffering, and maintain and protect human dignity during and after man-made crises and natural disasters. Such aid may also be used to prevent and strengthen preparedness for the occurrence of such situations.

indemnity insurance An insurance policy that pays claims based on the actual economic losses incurred by the policyholder.

index insurance An insurance policy that pays claims based on an index. Indexes are typically chosen to be a good proxy of the economic losses incurred by the policyholder.

individual loss adjustment The process by which a loss adjuster objectively assesses the actual damage for each insured building or injured person.

moral hazard In insurance, the problems generated when the insured's behaviour can influence the extent of damage that qualifies for insurance payouts. Examples of moral hazard are carelessness, fraudulent claims, and irresponsibility.

natural disaster An extreme event leading to loss of lives and livelihoods caused by natural hazards such as tropical cyclones, earthquakes, floods, and landslides.

parametric insurance A type of insurance that does not indemnify the pure loss but ex ante agrees to make a payment upon occurrence of a triggering event. The triggering event is often a catastrophic natural event, which may cause a loss.

post-disaster needs assessment A government-led exercise that assesses post-disaster needs with a view towards providing a platform for the international community to assist the affected government in recovery and reconstruction.

public financial management Steps taken to ensure that money is spent and accounted for in a clear and transparent fashion. A public financial management system comprises resource generation, resource allocation, and expenditure management (resource utilization).

Public Health Emergency of International Concern As defined in the International Health Regulations, 'an extraordinary event which is determined to constitute a public health risk to other States through the international spread of disease and to potentially require a coordinated international response'.

reinsurance A practice in which insurers transfer portions of risk portfolios to other parties in order to reduce the likelihood of having to pay a large obligation resulting from an insurance claim—that is, it is insurance of insurance.

risk-based pricing Pricing of an insurance policy to reflect the underlying risk that is transferred through the insurance contract.

risk pool An arrangement whereby several individuals, companies, or countries jointly insure against a certain pre-specified risk.

risk-retention instrument An instrument whereby a party retains the financial responsibility for loss in the event of a shock. Risk-retention instruments do not take risk off the balance sheet—the cost of a disaster must still be repaid. The instrument just offers more flexibility in how and when one would have to pay. Contingency funds, budget allocations, and lines of contingent credit are all risk-retention instruments, as are budget reallocations, tax increases, and post-disaster credit.

risk-transfer instrument An instrument, such as an insurance contract, that passes on the risks associated with a certain event from one party to another. For example, in disaster insurance the financial risks associated with a disaster event are passed from the insured to the insurer.

shock-responsive social protection Social protection that has the ability to increase its caseload and/or its intensity of support in response to catastrophic events.

status quo bias The tendency of people not to change what they are doing unless the incentive to do so is strong.

targeting The process of selecting beneficiaries under a social safety net programme.

trigger The event that must occur before a particular insurance policy applies to a given loss. For example, for weather-index insurance a trigger could be the weather measurement that causes the insurance policy to pay out, such as a certain amount of cumulative rainfall.

underwriting The process of issuing an insurance policy, thereby accepting a liability and guaranteeing payment in case a loss occurs.

NOTES

Chapter 1

1. Data on the exact impacts of disasters are always questionable, but various broadly reliable estimates exist. The data quoted here are from the EM-DAT (Emergency Events Database), <http://www.emdat.be>; Government of Haiti (2010); Government of Nepal (2015); Government of Pakistan (2011); and Swiss Re (2014). Germanwatch (2015) and UNISDR (2015) offer global estimates and discuss patterns of damage and loss of life.

2. In Somalia, it was not just the drought that mattered. The drought that peaked in 2011 killed tens of thousands in a large-scale famine that received a poor response. Some have suggested that up to 260,000 may have died, half of these young children (Checchi and Robinson 2013). But its impact was even more devastating because of the conflict raging in the country. Indeed, the droughts with the most devastating impacts in recent decades also took place during conflicts: for example, the drought and famine in Ethiopia in 1984–5 killed between 400,000 and a million people and caused long-term damage to people and their livelihoods (Dercon and Porter 2014). Other examples are Darfur in the 1980s, Ethiopia in 1972, and China (Henan) in 1942 or during the Great Leap Forward in 1958–61. The latter remains the largest famine in the last century; more than 15 million people died from starvation. It was a sign of progress in the latter half of the twentieth century that harvest failures only resulted in famines (defined as large-scale excess mortality) during conflict or serious political repression. See, for example, de Waal (2005) on Darfur in the 1980s, Wolde Mariam (1986) on Ethiopia in 1972–3, and Mitter (2013) on Henan, China, in 1942–3.

3. Hallegatte et al. (2015).

4. As of 2 December 2015, the World Health Organization reported 11,130 deaths in these three countries. See <http://apps.who.int/ebola/ebola-situation-reports>.

5. In this book, we use the shorthand 'natural disasters' to refer to disasters caused by extreme natural hazards. We recognize that extreme natural

hazards do not need to cause disasters and that human behaviour can increase or lessen the impact of these natural hazards (World Bank 2010).

6. More formal definitions are possible. ALNAP (2015: 18) refers to the 'network of interconnected institutional and operational entities through which humanitarian assistance is provided when local and national resources are insufficient to meet the needs of the affected population', and includes as actors UN humanitarian agencies, the International Red Cross and Red Crescent Movement, recipient government agencies, humanitarian arms of regional intergovernmental organizations, donor governments, and local, national, and international NGOs.

7. Details can be found in ALNAP, UKAid, and UNEG (2011).

8. See IASC (2014).

9. IASC (2014) discusses this in more detail.

10. More details can be found in Congressional Research Service (2006) and Department of Homeland Security (2006).

11. Many reports and analyses are devoted to discussing 'what went wrong' during the responses to disasters. A poorly planned and coordinated response is a common theme. Well-documented cases are the response to the 2010 Haiti earthquake—see, for example, ALNAP, UKAid, and UNEG (2011)—or the response to Typhoon Haiyan in the Philippines—see IASC (2014).

12. Strömberg (2007); World Bank (2014a).

13. See Congressional Research Service (2006) and Department of Homeland Security (2006).

14. Slater and Bhuvanendra (2014); Jensen et al. (2014).

15. Global Facility for Disaster Reduction and Recovery (2013).

16. Hoddinott et al. (2012); Slater and Bhuvanendra (2014).

17. UNISDR (2015).

18. According to Germanwatch (2015), in terms of extreme weather events poor developing countries are the most affected. Between 1994 and 2013, Honduras, Myanmar, and Haiti were the countries that suffered the most from extreme weather events. In 2013 the Philippines, Cambodia, and India led the list of such countries. Of the ten most affected countries from 1994 to 2013, nine were in the low-income or lower-middle-income country group, while only one was classified as an upper-middle-income country.

Chapter 2

1. The BBC website <http://www.bbc.com> stated on 26 April 2015 that 'a major earthquake has struck Nepal', 'hundreds of people are feared dead', and 'the government has declared a state of emergency in the affected areas'.

Soon the first appeals for assistance were heard. 'We need support from the various international agencies which are more knowledgeable and equipped to handle the kind of emergency we face now', said the Nepali information minister. *Time* magazine ran an article on 27 April entitled '6 Ways You Can Give to Nepal Earthquake Relief', giving details on six international charities. By 30 April, the BBC website was reporting more detailed estimates of damage and loss of lives: 'Officials say Saturday's quake killed more than 5,500 people, and injured at least 11,000. The UN says more than eight million people have been affected by Saturday's 7.8-magnitude quake and some 70,000 houses have been destroyed.' And the main appeal was reported: 'The UN has appealed for $415m (£270m) to help provide emergency relief over the next three months.'

2. On the 26 April, the BBC website reported that 'the [Nepali] government says it has been overwhelmed by the disaster'. By 28 April, the first fallout had begun: *Time* magazine reported under the headline 'Why Nepal Wasn't Ready for the Earthquake'. Documenting poor regulation and poor politics, it stated, 'People have been trying for a long time to improve preparedness and resilience, but they're resource-strapped.' By 30 April, the BBC website was reporting that 'survivors in some areas told the BBC that they were angry that neither food nor medicine has reached them'.

3. Clarke and Hill (2013); Cabot Venton et al. (2012).

4. Data from the Financial Tracking Service of the UN's Office for Coordination of Humanitarian Affairs (OCHA) suggested that in December 2015 there were twenty-four live appeals for Humanitarian Response Plans, as well as six Refugee Response Plans and a number of flash appeals. The total appeals were for just under US$20 billion, of which just 50 per cent were either paid or committed via pledges by donors. Several of the largest involved conflict-related crises (such as Syria or the Democratic Republic of Congo), but large appeals also included the Nepal earthquake ($420 million, of which $150 million has been unmet), and more than $1.4 billion in total for Burkina Faso, Mali, Chad, and Niger, much of it related to drought, floods, and other extreme events. Of that $1.4 billion, $850 million was unmet.

5. See Congressional Research Service (2006) or Department of Homeland Security (2006).

6. WHO (2015).

7. Kucharski et al. (2015).

8. Procrastination could be related to different cognitive biases commonly found in people (Samuelson and Zeckhauser 1988). Ritov and Baron (1992) distinguish between status quo bias (explained by loss aversion) and

omission bias (explained by a failure to act, which arises through a failure to see the possibility of action). See <https://fts.unocha.org/reports/daily/ocha_R21_Y2015_asof___4_December_2015_(02_31).pdf>. O'Donoghue and Rabin (1999) discuss explanations linked to self-control problems.

9. Bailey (2013).
10. For example, on 28 June 2011, Reuters reported, 'Worst drought in 60 years hitting Horn of Africa: U.N.'. The UK's Channel 4 news website stated, 'East African drought worst in 60 years'. On 22 October 2011, the *Independent* in the UK wrote, 'Africa's worst drought in 60 years threatens famine...'.
11. Bailey (2013).
12. See Sen (1983) for an early articulation or Sen (2009) for a recent discussion. Sen suggested that the 1958–61 famine during the Great Leap Forward in China happened because news was repressed, and so news of the famine did not even reach the top party leadership. India has been able to avoid famines since independence because a free press and the pressures of elections have meant that politicians have been held accountable for responding to disasters.
13. Besley and Burgess (2002).
14. Sainath (2000).
15. Cole et al. (2012).
16. Gasper and Reeves (2011); Reeves (2011).
17. Healy and Malhotra (2009).
18. Rutherford (2001).
19. Rutherford (2001).
20. Dercon et al. (2006).
21. Historically, fire insurance was also the first commercial product targeting households to emerge. A few years after the catastrophic Great Fire of London in 1666, the Insurance Office for Houses, probably the first fire-insurance company, was founded. It was set up as a mutual fund, pooling the contributions of its members, with payouts further guaranteed by a property-investment portfolio. Recognizing the benefits of preparedness, this company and its fast-emerging competitors ended up setting up the first fire brigades, offering protection to the properties they insured and only those.

Chapter 3

1. Congressional Research Service (2006); Department of Homeland Security (2006).
2. <http://www.usnews.com/opinion/blogs/world-report/2015/05/07/nepal-earthquake-response-shows-need-for-better-international-planning>.

3. <http://www.irinnews.org/Report/102244/Nepal-unlocks-quake-funds-It-only-took-7-months>.
4. Kucharski et al. (2015).
5. Clarke and Hill (2013). Cabot Venton et al. (2012) suggest even higher figures for Ethiopia and double the cost of a late response in Kenya compared with an early response.
6. Tversky and Kahneman (1974) first suggested that this is a cognitive bias, resulting in deviations in rational decision making.
7. 'Build back better' is now recognized as good practice globally, having gained momentum following the 2004 Indian Ocean tsunami and as one of the four priorities for action under the Sendai Framework for Disaster Risk Reduction.
8. For a review of health interventions during humanitarian interventions, see Blanchet et al. (2015). Of the 131 studies of sufficient quality that could be included, only 10 per cent took place in the settings of disasters caused by natural events.
9. For one recent review of the challenges of—but also opportunities for—better evaluations in humanitarian settings, see Puri et al. (2015).
10. Financial contracts are not always necessary. One informative counterexample is Japan, where the government signed a contingent service contract with a construction company for post-disaster reconstruction. Through this and similar contracts, key highways were rebuilt within two weeks of the Tōhoku earthquake and tsunami in 2011.
11. See de Janvry et al. (2015).

Chapter 4

1. Trenerry (1926).
2. Rutherford (2001); Dercon et al. (2006); Roth (2001); Thomson and Posel (2002).
3. Madrian and Shea (2001) show this for US retirement savings products.
4. Bryan et al. (2010).
5. Samuelson and Zeckhauser (1988).
6. Madrian and Shea (2001).
7. Thaler and Sunstein (2008); Goldstein et al. (2008).
8. Simon (1956); Kahneman (2011); Thaler and Sunstein (2008).
9. Gigerenzer and Goldstein (1996).
10. An alternative approach would be to use rules to trigger financing but leave the prioritization until after the disaster—for example, to be decided under a

clear accountability and decision-making framework using information from a Post Disaster Needs Assessment (PDNA).

11. Dercon (2005).

12. A careful review of the relevant evidence that comes out in strong support of using more cash in humanitarian aid is Overseas Development Institute and Centre for Global Development (2015).

13. Some issues have to be monitored when moving to cash. One is that cash transfers retain their value. Therefore, if prices increase, the value of the transfers needs to be adjusted in a reasonable way to keep purchasing power constant. Also, food supplies need to be guaranteed, but this is about monitoring markets and potentially promoting or supporting imports, not necessarily delivering food to people directly.

14. For example, the Japanese earthquake and tsunami early warning system saved thousands of lives in the aftermath of the 2011 Tōhoku earthquake and tsunami by enabling high-speed trains to be slowed so that they did not derail, dangerous machinery to be shut off so it did not cause damage, and people to find cover or move to high ground so they were not injured or killed. See 'How Japan's Rail Network Survived the Earthquake', *Railway Technology*, <http://www.railway-technology.com/features/feature122751/>.

15. WHO (2015).

16. Bailey (2013).

17. For some of the experiences related to RISEPAK during the 2005 Kashmir earthquake, see <http://en.wikipedia.org/wiki/RISE-PAK> and RISEPAK (2005).

18. Bailey (2013).

Chapter 5

1. Kirkwood (2009).

2. World Bank (2012).

3. A reinsurance policy is essentially an insurance policy for insurers. A catastrophe bond is an insurance-linked security in which payment of interest or principal is suspended or cancelled in the event of a specified catastrophe, such as an earthquake.

4. Munich Re (2013).

5. Beyond insurance, there are other insights from finance that are relevant to financial planning for disasters. For example, if a plan requires delivering grain to drought-stricken individuals it would be important to manage both price and quantity risks. Price risk is typically best implemented through

dynamic financial management where a portfolio of financial instruments is actively rebalanced as time passes and prices change to hedge the price risk.

6. For a more comprehensive description of financial and budgetary instruments available to governments for financing disaster risk, see Cummins and Mahul (2009).

7. Authors' calculations based on data from the Financial Tracking Service (FTS) of the UN's Office for Coordination of Humanitarian Affairs (OCHA), <https://fts.unocha.org>.

8. Insurance and reinsurance prices are typically the result of a negotiation. Risk-reduction investments will not automatically reduce the cost of insurance and reinsurance, but, if well explained in these negotiations, they should typically result in premium reductions.

9. Captive insurance companies are insurance companies established by a parent company with the specific objective of covering the risks to which the parent is exposed.

10. For the general principle, see Arrow (1963); for the case of disaster risk financing for governments, see Clarke et al. (2015).

11. Jensen et al. (2014).

12. Hoddinott et al. (2012).

13. Cabinet Decree No. 17 of June 5, 1991 (Panama), Supreme Decree 007-2008-Housing (Peru), and Article 48, paragraph 63 of Law 734 of 2002 (Colombia).

14. Specific examples are France's Catastrophe Naturelles, the Japanese Earthquake Reinsurance Company, the New Zealand Earthquake Commission, Norway's Norsk Naturskadepool, Spain's Consorcio de Compensacion de Seguros, the Florida Hurricane Catastrophe Fund, the Hawaii Hurricane Relief Fund, the California Earthquake Authority, the Taiwan Residential Earthquake Insurance Pool, and the Turkish Catastrophic Insurance Pool (TCIP). See Cummins and Mahul (2009).

15. Following the 2011 Christchurch earthquake, which caused about US$17 billion in insured losses, the government of New Zealand injected further capital into the New Zealand Earthquake Commission, an earthquake reinsurer guaranteed by the government, to enable it to pay about half of the total claims (see <http://www.eqc.govt.nz/canterbury-earthquakes/progress-updates/scorecard>). It also bailed out the second-largest insurance company in the country, AMI Insurance (Muir-Wood 2012). Following Hurricane Wilma, which struck Florida in 2005, the Poe Financial Group declared insolvency, and claims had to be paid by the state-sponsored reinsurer, the Florida Hurricane Catastrophe Fund, and by the state-sponsored

insurer of last resort, the Citizens Property Insurance Company (Linnerooth-Bayer et al. 2011).

16. Mahul and Stutley (2010).

17. There are some exceptions, however. The Turkish government established a compulsory, unsubsidized earthquake insurance pool for homeowners' buildings, and the combination of compulsion and clever, well-funded awareness-raising has led to some 6.8 million buildings being insured (TCIP 2013) out of a total of 19.5 billion, with owners paying the full cost of earthquake insurance themselves (Turkish Statistical Institute 2013).

18. Cat DDOs are in place in ten countries for a total value of US$1.38 billion: $7 million to the Seychelles in 2014; $102 million to Sri Lanka in 2014; $250 million to Colombia in 2011; $50 million to El Salvador in 2011; $66 million to Panama in 2011; $500 million to the Philippines in 2011; $100 million to Peru in 2010; $85 million to Guatemala in 2009; $150 million to Colombia in 2008; and $65 million to Costa Rica in 2008.

19. The premium for Haiti was paid for the 2015–16 season through a grant provided by the Caribbean Development Bank. All other Caribbean countries paid the full premium themselves. Nicaragua paid the premium through a concessionary loan from the International Development Association (IDA), the World Bank fund for the poorest countries. Since its inception, CCRIF has paid thirteen claims totalling US$38 million.

20. For 2015–16, the Cook Islands, Republic of the Marshall Islands, Samoa, Tonga, and Vanuatu all purchased parametric catastrophe insurance coverage against major tropical cyclones and earthquakes (including tsunami). Since its inception, the PCRAFI has paid two claims totalling US$3.2 million.

21. For 2014–15, Kenya, Mauritania, Niger, and Senegal all purchased parametric insurance coverage against drought. Since its inception, the ARC has paid three claims totalling US$25 million.

22. UN OCHA FTS data.

23. Murtaza (2015).

REFERENCES

Alderman, H., and T. Haque. 2007. 'Insurance against Covariate Shocks: The Role of Index-Based Insurance in Social Protection in Low-Income Countries of Africa'. Working Paper No. 95, World Bank, Washington.

Alderman, Harold, John Hoddinott, and Bill Kinsey. 2003. 'Long-Term Consequences of Early Childhood Malnutrition'. IFPRI Discussion Paper No. 168, Food Consumption and Nutrition Division, International Food Policy Research Institute, Washington.

ALNAP. 2015. *The State of the Humanitarian System.* ALNAP Study. London: ALNAP/ODI.

ALNAP, UKAid, and UNEG. 2011. 'Evaluation Insights: Haiti Earthquake Responses—Emerging Evaluation Lessons'. June.

Armendáriz, B., and J. Morduch. 2010. *The Economics of Microfinance.* Cambridge: MIT Press.

Arrow, K. J. 1971. *Essays in the Theory of Risk-Bearing.* Amsterdam: North-Holland.

Arrow, Kenneth. 1963. 'Uncertainty and the Welfare Economics of Medical Care'. *American Economic Review* 53: 941.

Arrow, Kenneth, and Robert C. Lind. 1970. 'Uncertainty and the Evaluation of Public Investment Decisions'. *American Economic Review* 60: 364.

Ashraf, Nava, Dean Karlan, and Wesley Yin. 2006. 'Tying Odysseus to the Mast: Evidence from a Commitment Savings Product in the Philippines'. *Quarterly Journal of Economics* 121: 635.

Bailey, Rob. 2013. *Managing Famine Risk: Linking Early Warning to Early Action.* Chatham House Report. London: Royal Institute of International Affairs, April.

Barnett, Barry J., Christopher B. Barrett, and Jeremy R. Skees. 2008. 'Poverty Traps and Index-Based Risk Transfer Products'. *World Development* 36: 1766.

Bastagli, Francesca, and Luke Hardman. 2015. *The Role of Index-Based Triggers in Social Protection Shock Response.* London: Overseas Development Institute.

Bastagli, F., and R. Holmes. 2014. *Delivering Social Protection in the Aftermath of a Shock: Lessons from Bangladesh, Kenya, Pakistan and Viet Nam.* London: Overseas Development Institute.

Berg, M. A., R. Portillo, M. E. F. Buffie, M. C. A. Pattillo, and L. F. Zanna. 2012. 'Public Investment, Growth, and Debt Sustainability: Putting Together the Pieces'. Working Paper No. 12–144, International Monetary Fund, Washington.

Besley, Timothy, and Robin Burgess. 2002. 'The Political Economy of Government Responsiveness: Theory and Evidence from India'. *Quarterly Journal of Economics* 117: 1415.

Bevan, David, and Christopher Adam. 2015. 'Public Capital, Disaster Risk Insurance and Macroeconomic Responses to Topical Cyclone Damage: An Application to Jamaica'. Oxford University.

Bharosa, Nitesh, JinKyu Lee, and Marijn Janssen. 2010. 'Challenges and Obstacles in Sharing and Coordinating Information during Multi-Agency Disaster Response: Propositions from Field Exercises'. *Information Systems Frontiers* 12: 49.

Blanchet, K., et al. 2015. 'An Evidence Review of Research on Health Interventions in Humanitarian Crises'. London School of Hygiene and Tropical Medicine.

Borch, K. 1962. 'Equilibrium in a Reinsurance Market'. *Econometrica: Journal of the Econometric Society* 30: 424.

Browne, Mark J., and Robert E. Hoyt. 2000. 'The Demand for Flood Insurance: Empirical Evidence'. *Journal of Risk and Uncertainty* 20: 291.

Bryan, Gharad, Dean Karlan, and Scott Nelson. 2010. 'Commitment Devices'. *Annual Review of Economics* 2: 671.

Buchanan, James M. 1975. 'The Samaritan's Dilemma'. In *Altruism, Morality and Economic Theory*, edited by Edmund S. Phelps. New York: Russell Sage Foundation, 71.

Buzzacchi, L., and G. Turati. 2014. 'Optimal Risk Allocation in the Provision of Local Public Services: Can a Private Insurer Be Better than a Federal Relief Fund?' *CESifo Economic Studies*, ifu024.

Cabot Venton, Courtenay, Catherine Fitzgibbon, Tenna Shitarek, Lorraine Coulter, and Olivia Dooley. 2012. 'The Economics of Early Response and Disaster Resilience: Lessons from Kenya and Ethiopia'. Economics of Resilience Final Report, UK Department for International Development, London.

Carter, M. 2013. 'Sharing the Risk and the Uncertainty: Public–Private Reinsurance Partnerships for Viable Agricultural Insurance Markets'. *I4 Index Insurance Innovation Initiative Brief*, 1.

Carter, M., A. de Janvry, E. Sadoulet, and A. Sarris. 2014. 'Index-Based Weather Insurance for Developing Countries: A Review of Evidence and a Set of Propositions for Up-scaling'. Ferdi Document de travail P111.

Carter, M. R., F. Galarza, and S. Boucher. 2007. 'Underwriting Area-Based Yield Insurance to Crowd-In Credit Supply and Demand'. *Savings and Development* 31: 335.

Caunhye, Aakil M., Xiaofeng Nie, and Shaligram Pokharel. 2012. 'Optimization Models in Emergency Logistics: A Literature Review'. *Socio-Economic Planning Sciences* 46: 4.

Chakravarti, J. S. 1920. *Agricultural Insurance: A Practical Scheme Suited to Indian Conditions.* Bangalore: Government Press.

Chantarat, S., C. B. Barrett, A. G. Mude, and C. G. Turvey. 2007. 'Using Weather Index Insurance to Improve Drought Response for Famine Prevention'. *American Journal of Agricultural Economics* 89: 1262.

Chantarat, S., A. G. Mude, C. B. Barrett, and M. R. Carter. 2009. 'Designing Index-based Livestock Insurance for Managing Asset Risk in Northern Kenya'. *Journal of Risk and Insurance* 80: 205.

Charpentier, A., and B. Le Maux. 2014. 'Natural Catastrophe Insurance: How Should the Government Intervene?' *Journal of Public Economics* 115: 1.

Checchi, Francesco, and W. Courtland Robinson. 2013. 'Mortality among Populations of Southern and Central Somalia Affected by Severe Food Insecurity and Famine during 2010–2012'. A study commissioned by FAO/FSNAU and FEWS NET from the London School of Hygiene and Tropical Medicine and the Johns Hopkins University Bloomberg School of Public Health.

Christopher, Martin, and Peter Tatham, eds. 2014. *Humanitarian Logistics—Meeting the Challenge of Preparing for and Responding to Disasters.* London: Kogan Page Publishers.

Clarke, D. J. 2016. 'A Theory of Rational Demand for Index Insurance'. *American Economic Journal: Microeconomics* 8: 1.

Clarke, D. J., O. Mahul, and P. Poulter. 2015. 'A Framework for the Ex Ante Evaluation of Alternative Sovereign Disaster Risk Financing Strategies'. World Bank, Washington.

Clarke, D., O. Mahul, K. N. Rao, and N. Verma. 2012. 'Weather Based Crop Insurance in India'. Policy Research Working Paper 5985, World Bank, Washington.

Clarke, Daniel J., and Ruth Vargas Hill. 2013. 'Cost-Benefit Analysis of the African Risk Capacity Facility'. Discussion Paper 01292, International Food Policy Research Institute, Washington.

Coate, S. 1995. 'Altruism, the Samaritan's Dilemma, and Government Transfer Policy'. *American Economic Review* 85: 46.

Cohen, Charles, and Eric D. Werker. 2008. 'The Political Economy of "Natural" Disasters'. *Journal of Conflict Resolution* 52: 795.

Cole, Shawn, Xavier Giné, Jeremy Tobacman, Petia Topalova, Robert Townsend, and James Vickery. 2013. 'Barriers to Household Risk Management: Evidence from India'. *American Economic Journal: Applied Economics* 5: 104.

Cole, S., A. Healy, and E. Werker. 2012. 'Do Voters Demand Responsive Governments? Evidence from Indian Disaster Relief'. *Journal of Development Economics* 97: 167.

Cole, S., D. Stein, and J. Tobacman. 2014. 'Dynamics and Demand for Index Insurance: Evidence from a Long-Run Field Experiment'. *American Economic Review: Papers and Proceedings* 104: 284.

Congressional Research Service. 2006. 'Federal Emergency Management Policy Changes after Hurricane Katrina: A Summary of Statutory Provisions'. CRS Report for Congress, Library of Congress, Washington.

Cummins, J. David, and Olivier Mahul. 2009. *Catastrophe Risk Financing in Developing Countries: Principles for Public Intervention*. Washington: World Bank.

Debreu, G. 1954. 'Valuation Equilibrium and Pareto Optimum'. *Proceedings of the National Academy of Sciences of the United States of America* 40: 588.

de Janvry, Alain, Alejandro del Valle, and Elisabeth Sadoulet. 2015. 'Insuring Growth: The Impact of Disaster Funds on Economic Reconstruction'. Department of Agricultural and Resource Economics, University of California, Berkeley.

Department of Homeland Security. 2006. 'A Performance Review of FEMA's Disaster Management Activities in Response to Hurricane Katrina'. Office of Inspector General, Washington.

Dercon, Stefan. 2004. 'Growth and Shocks: Evidence from Rural Ethiopia'. *Journal of Development Economics* 74: 309.

Dercon, Stefan. 2005. *Insurance against Poverty*. Oxford: Oxford University Press.

Dercon, S., J. De Weerdt, T. Bold, and A. Pankhurst. 2006. 'Group-Based Funeral Insurance in Ethiopia and Tanzania'. *World Development* 34: 685.

Dercon, Stefan, and Catherine Porter. 2014. 'Live Aid Revisited'. *Journal of the European Economic Association* 12: 927.

de Waal, Alex. 2005. *Famine that Kills: Darfur, Sudan*. Rev. ed. Oxford: Oxford University Press.

Eisensee, Thomas, and David Strömberg. 2007. 'News Floods, News Droughts, and U.S. Disaster Relief'. *Quarterly Journal of Economics* 122: 693.

Elabed, Ghada, and Michael R. Carter. 2014. 'Ex-ante Impacts of Agricultural Insurance: Evidence from a Field Experiment in Mali'. University of California, Davis.

Estache, A., and L. Wren-Lewis. 2009. 'Toward a Theory of Regulation for Developing Countries: Following Jean-Jacques Laffont's Lead'. *Journal of Economic Literature* 47: 729.

Fuchs, Alan, and Lourdes Rodriguez-Chamussy. 2014. 'Voter Response to Natural Disaster Aid: Quasi-Experimental Evidence from Drought Relief Payments in Mexico'. Policy Research Working Paper 6836, World Bank, Washington.

Fuchs, Alan, and Hendrik Wolff. 2011. 'Concept and Unintended Consequences of Weather Index Insurance: The Case of Mexico'. *American Journal of Agricultural Economics* 93: 505.

Gasper, J., and A. Reeves. 2011. 'Make it Rain? Retrospection and the Attentive Electorate in the Context of Natural Disasters'. *American Journal of Political Science* 55: 340.

Gawande, A. 2010. *The Checklist Manifesto: How to Get Things Right*. New York: Metropolitan Books.

Germanwatch. 2015. 'Global Climate Risk Index 2015'. <https://germanwatch.org/en/cri>.

Ghesquiere, Francis, and Olivier Mahul. 2007. 'Sovereign Natural Disaster Insurance for Developing Countries: A Paradigm Shift in Catastrophe Risk Financing'. Policy Research Working Paper 4345, World Bank, Washington.

Gigerenzer, Gerd, and Daniel G. Goldstein. 1996. 'Reasoning the Fast and Frugal Way: Models of Bounded Rationality'. *Psychological Review* 103: 650.

Global Facility for Disaster Reduction and Recovery. 2013. *FONDEN: Mexico's National Disaster Fund*. World Bank, Washington.

Goldstein, D. G., E. J. Johnson, A. Herrmann, and M. Heitmann. 2008. 'Nudge Your Customers toward Better Choices'. *Harvard Business Review* 86: 99.

Gollier, C. 2003. 'To Insure or Not to Insure? An Insurance Puzzle'. *Geneva Papers on Risk and Insurance Theory* 28: 5.

Government of Haiti. 2010. 'Haiti Earthquake PDNA: Assessment of Damage, Losses, General and Sectoral Needs'. Port-au-Prince.

Government of Nepal. 2015. *Nepal Earthquake 2015 Post Disaster Needs Assessment. Vol. A: Key Findings*. Kathmandu: Government of Nepal National Planning Commission.

Government of Pakistan. 2011. '2011 Pakistan Floods: Preliminary Damage and Needs Assessment'. Government of Pakistan, World Bank, and Asian Development Bank.

Grosh, M., C. Andrews, R. Quintana, and C. Rodriguez-Alas. 2011. 'Assessing Safety Net Readiness in Response to Food Price Volatility'. Social Protection Discussion Paper 1118, Social Protection and Labour, World Bank, Washington, September.

Gurenko, Eugene, Rodney Lester, Olivier Mahul, and Serap Oguz Gonulal. 2006. *Earthquake Insurance in Turkey: History of the Turkish Catastrophe Insurance Pool*. Washington: World Bank.

Hallegatte, Stephane, Mook Bangalore, Laura Bonzanigo, Marianne Fay, Tamaro Kane, Ulf Narloch, Julie Rozenberg, David Treguer, and Adrien Vogt-Schilb. 2015. *Shock Waves: Managing the Impacts of Climate Change on Poverty*. Washington: World Bank.

Hazell, P. B. 1992. 'The Appropriate Role of Agricultural Insurance in Developing Countries'. *Journal of International Development* 4: 567.

Healy, A., and N. Malhotra. 2009. 'Myopic Voters and Natural Disaster Policy'. *American Political Science Review* 103: 387.

Hess, U., J. R. Skees, A. Stoppa, B. J. Barnett, and J. Nash. 2005. *Managing Agricultural Production Risk: Innovations in Developing Countries*. Washington: World Bank.

Hill, R. V, G. Gajate-Garrido, C. Phily, and A. Dalal. 2014. 'Using Subsidies for Inclusive Insurance: Lessons from Agriculture and Health'. Microinsurance Innovation Facility Paper, 29, International Labour Organization, Geneva.

Hobson, M., and L. Campbell. 2012. 'How Ethiopia's Productive Safety Net Programme (PSNP) Is Responding to the Current Humanitarian Crisis in the Horn'. *Humanitarian Exchange* 53.

Hoddinott, John, Guush Berhane, Daniel O. Gilligan, Neha Kumar, and Alemayehu Seyoum Taffesse. 2012. 'The Impact of Ethiopia's Productive Safety Net Programme and Related Transfers on Agricultural Productivity'. *Journal of African Economies* 21: 761.

Hölmstrom, B. 1979. 'Moral Hazard and Observability'. *Bell Journal of Economics* 10: 74.

Hsiang, S. M., and D. Narita. 2012. 'Adaptation to Cyclone Risk: Evidence from the Global Cross-Section'. *Climate Change Economics* 3: 1.

IASC (Inter-Agency Standing Committee). 2014. 'Inter-Agency Humanitarian Evaluation of the Typhoon Haiyan Response'. Prepared on behalf of the Inter-Agency Humanitarian Evaluation Steering Group, October.

Jaffee, D., and T. Russell. 2013. 'The Welfare Economics of Catastrophe Losses and Insurance'. *Geneva Papers on Risk and Insurance-Issues and Practice* 38: 469.

Janssen, Marijn, JinKyu Lee, Nitesh Nharosa, and Anthony Cresswell. 2010. 'Advances in Multi-Agency Disaster Management: Key Elements in Disaster Research'. *Information Systems Frontiers* 12: 1.

Janzen, S. A., and M. R. Carter. 2013. *After the Drought: The Impact of Microinsurance on Consumption Smoothing and Asset Protection*. NBER Report No. w19702, National Bureau of Economic Research, Cambridge.

Jensen, Nathaniel Duane, Christopher B. Barrett, and Andrew Mude. 2014. 'Basis Risk and the Welfare Gains from Index Insurance: Evidence from

Northern Kenya'. Department of Applied Economics and Management, Cornell University, Ithaca, December 10.

Kahneman, D. 2011. *Thinking, Fast and Slow*. New York: Farrar, Straus and Giroux.

Kahneman, D., J. L. Knetsch, and R. H. Thaler. 1991. 'Anomalies: The Endowment Effect, Loss Aversion, and Status Quo Bias'. *Journal of Economic Perspectives* 5: 193.

Kaplow, L. 1991. 'Incentives and Government Relief for Risk'. *Journal of Risk and Uncertainty* 4: 167.

Kapucu, Naim. 2006. 'Interagency Communication Networks during Emergencies—Boundary Spanners in Multiagency Coordination'. *American Review of Public Administration* 36: 207.

Karlan, Dean, Robert Darko Osei, Isaac Osei-Akoto, and Christopher Udry. 2012. 'Agricultural Decisions after Relaxing Credit and Risk Constraints'. NBER Working Paper 18463, National Bureau of Economic Research, Cambridge.

Kirkwood, J. B. 2009. *The History of Mexico*. Santa Barbara: ABC-CLIO.

Kousky, C., E. O. Michel-Kerjan, and P. Raschky. 2013. 'Does Federal Disaster Assistance Crowd Out Private Demand for Insurance?' Risk Management and Decision Processes Center, The Wharton School, University of Pennsylvania.

Kucharski, Adam J., Anton Camacho, Stefan Flasche, Rebecca E. Glover, W. John Edmunds, and Sebastian Fund. 2015. 'Measuring the Impact of Ebola Control Measures in Sierra Leone'. *Proceedings of the National Academy of Sciences of the United States* 112: 14366.

Kunreuther, Howard. 2015. 'The Role of Insurance in Reducing Losses from Extreme Events: The Need for Public–Private Partnerships'. *Geneva Risk and Insurance Review* 4: 741.

Kunreuther, Howard C., and E. O. Michel-Kerjan. 2009. *At War with the Weather: Managing Large-Scale Risks in a New Era of Catastrophes*. Cambridge: MIT Press.

Kunreuther, Howard, and M. Pauly. 2006. 'Rules Rather than Discretion: Lessons from Hurricane Katrina'. *Journal of Risk and Uncertainty* 33: 101.

Kydland, Finn E., and Edward C. Prescott. 1977. 'Rules Rather than Discretion: The Inconsistency of Optimal Plans'. *Journal of Political Economy* 85: 473.

Lacker, J. M., and J. A. Weinberg. 1989. 'Optimal Contracts under Costly State Falsification'. *Journal of Political Economy* 97: 1345–63.

Lam, J. 2014. *Enterprise Risk Management: From Incentives to Controls*. Hoboken: John Wiley.

Ley-Borrás, R., and B. D. Fox. 2015. 'Using Probabilistic Models to Appraise and Decide on Sovereign Disaster Risk Financing and Insurance'. Policy Research Working Paper 7358, World Bank, Washington.

Lindbeck, A., and J. W. Weibull. 1988. 'Altruism and Time Consistency: The Economics of Fait Accompli'. *Journal of Political Economy* 96: 1165.

Linnerooth-Bayer, J., R. Mechler, and S. Hochrainer. 2011. 'Insurance against Losses from Natural Disasters in Developing Countries. Evidence, Gaps and the Way Forward'. *IDRiM Journal* 1: 59.

Lucas, Robert E., Jr. 1976. 'Econometric Policy Evaluation: A Critique'. *Carnegie-Rochester Conference Series on Public Policy* 1: 19.

Madrian, B., and D. Shea. 2001. 'The Power of Suggestion: Inertia in 401(k) Participation and Savings Behavior'. *Quarterly Journal of Economics* 116: 1149.

Mahul, Olivier, and Charles Stutley. 2010. *Government Support to Agricultural Insurance: Challenges and Options for Developing Countries.* Washington: World Bank.

McCulloch, S., J. Skees, J. Hartell, D. Bierenbaum, B. Collier, and S. Young. 2015. *Disaster Resilient Microfinance: A New Model for Disaster Preparedness and Response for Microfinance Institutions.* London: UKAid, World Vision, Vision Fund International.

Mitter, Rana. 2013. *Forgotten Ally: China's World War II 1937–1945.* Boston: Houghton Mifflin Harcourt.

Mobarak, Ahmed Mushfiq, and Mark R. Rosenzweig. 2012. 'Selling Formal Insurance to the Informally Insured'. Yale Economics Department Working Paper No. 97; Yale University Economic Growth Center Discussion Paper No. 1007, Yale University, New Haven, February 1.

Morsink, K. 2015. 'Redistribution and Implicit Punishment. Experimental Evidence from Ethiopian Farmers' Risk-Taking Decisions'. Department of Economics, University of Oxford.

Muir-Wood, Robert. 2012. 'The Christchurch Earthquakes of 2010 and 2011'. *Geneva Reports* 5.

Munich Re. 2013. *Claims Management Following Natural Catastrophes.* Munich: Munich Re.

Murtaza, N. 2015. *Second Independent Evaluation of the Start Fund.* London: Start Network.

Nocco, Brian W., and René M. Stulz. 2006. 'Enterprise Risk Management: Theory and Practice'. *Journal of Applied Corporate Finance* 18: 8.

O'Donoghue, T., and M. Rabin. 1999. 'Doing It Now or Later'. *American Economic Review* 89: 103.

Osborne, M. J., and A. Rubinstein. 1990. *Bargaining and Markets.* San Diego: Academic Press.

Overseas Development Institute and Centre for Global Development. 2015. 'Doing Cash Differently. How Cash Transfers Can Transform Humanitarian Aid. Report of the High Level Panel on Humanitarian Cash Transfers'. London.

Pelham, L., E. Clay, and T. Braunholz. 2011. 'Natural Disasters: What Is the Role for Social Safety Nets?' Social Protection Discussion Paper No. 1102, Social Protection and Labour, World Bank, Washington.

Phaup, Marvin, and Charlotte Kirschner. 2010. 'Budgeting for Disasters: Focusing on the Good Times'. *OECD Journal on Budgeting* 10/1.

Picard, P. 2008. 'Natural Disaster Insurance and the Equity–Efficiency Trade-Off'. *Journal of Risk and Insurance* 75: 17.

Pomeroy, G. 2010. Testimony before the House Committee on Financial Services. Hearing on Approaches to Mitigating and Managing Natural Catastrophe Risk, H.R. 2555, Homeowners' Defense Act, 111th Cong., 2nd Sess., 10 March.

Pronovost, Peter, et al. 2006. 'An Intervention to Decrease Catheter-Related Bloodstream Infections in the ICU'. *New England Journal of Medicine* 355: 2725.

Puri, Jyotsna, Anastasia Aladysheva, Vegard Iversen, Yashodhan Ghorp, and Tilman Bruck. 2015. 'What Methods May Be Used in Impact Evaluations of Humanitarian Assistance?' IZA Discussion Paper 8755, Institute for the Study of Labor, Bonn, January.

Raschky, Paul A., and Hannelore Weck-Hannemann. 2007. 'Charity Hazard: A Real Hazard to Natural Disaster Insurance?' Working Papers in Economics and Statistics No. 2007–04, Faculty of Economics and Statistics, University of Innsbruck.

Reeves, A. 2011. 'Political Disaster: Unilateral Powers, Electoral Incentives, and Presidential Disaster Declarations'. *Journal of Politics* 73: 1142.

RISEPAK (Relief Information System for Earthquakes—Pakistan). 2005. 'Coordinating Disaster Relief Efforts: A New Tool for Relief Operations in Pakistan'. Center for International Development at Harvard University, Cambridge, MA <http://cid.harvard.edu>.

Ritov, I., and J. Baron. 1992. 'Status-Quo and Omission Biases'. *Journal of Risk and Uncertainty* 5: 49.

Roth J. 2001. 'Informal Microinsurance Schemes—The Case of Funeral Insurance in South Africa'. *Small Enterprise Development* 12: 39.

Rutherford, S. 2001. *The Poor and Their Money.* Oxford: Oxford India Paperbacks, Oxford University Press.

Sainath, Palagummi. 2000. *Stories from India's Poorest Districts.* London: Penguin Books.

Samuelson, William, and Richard Zeckhauser. 1988. 'Status Quo Bias in Decision Making'. *Journal of Risk and Uncertainty* 1: 7.

Sen, Amartya. 1983. 'Development: Which Way Now?' *Economic Journal* 93: 745.

Sen, Amartya. 2009. *The Idea of Justice*. London: Allen Lane.

Simon, Herbert A. 1956. 'Rational Choice and the Structure of the Environment'. *Psychological Review* 63: 129.

Skees, J., P. B. Hazell, and M. Miranda. 1999. 'New Approaches to Crop Yield Insurance in Developing Countries'. No. 55, International Food Policy Research Institute, Washington.

Slater, R., and D. Bhuvanendra. 2014. 'Scaling Up Existing Social Safety Nets to Provide Humanitarian Response: A Case Study of Ethiopia's Productive Safety Net Programme and Kenya's Hunger Safety Net Programme'. Fit for the Future Social Protection Thematic Study, Cash Learning Partnership (CaLP).

Stephenson, Max. 2005. 'Making Humanitarian Relief Networks More Effective: Operational Coordination, Trust and Sense-Making'. *Disasters* 29: 337.

Strömberg, D. 2007. 'Natural Disasters, Economic Development, and Humanitarian Aid'. *Journal of Economic Perspectives* 21: 199.

Swiss Re. 2014. 'Natural Catastrophes and Man-Made Disasters in 2013: Large Losses from Floods and Hail; Haiyan Hits the Philippines'. *Sigma* 1/2014.

Swiss Re. 2015. 'Natural Catastrophes and Man-Made Disasters in 2014: Convective and Winter Storms Generate Most Losses'. *Sigma* (February).

Taylor, John B. 1993. 'Discretion versus Policy Rules in Practice'. *Carnegie-Rochester Conference Series on Public Policy* 39: 195.

TCIP (Turkish Catastrophe Insurance Pool). 2013. Doğal Afet Sigortalari Kurumu Zorunlu Deprem Sigortasi Faaliyet Raporu.

Thaler, R., and S. Bernatzi. 2004. 'Save More Tomorrow: Using Behavioral Economics to Increase Employee Saving'. *Journal of Political Economy* 112: S164.

Thaler, Richard, and Cass Sunstein. 2008. *Nudge: Improving Decisions About Health, Wealth and Happiness*. New Haven: Yale University Press.

Thomson, R. J., and D. B. Posel. 2002. 'The Management of Risk by Burial Societies in South Africa'. *South African Actuarial Journal* 2: 83.

Townsend, R. M. 1979. 'Optimal Contracts and Competitive Markets with Costly State Verification'. *Journal of Economic Theory* 21: 265.

Trenerry, C. F. 1926. *The Origin and Early History of Insurance: Including the Contract of Bottomry*. London: P. S. King and Son.

Turkish Statistical Institute. 2013. 'Population and Housing Census, 2011'. News release no. 15843, 31 January.

Tversky, Amos, and Daniel Kahneman. 1974. 'Judgment under Uncertainty: Heuristics and Biases'. *Science* 185: 1124.

UNISDR (United Nations Office for Disaster Risk Reduction). 2011. *Global Assessment Report on Disaster Risk Reduction 2011: Revealing Risk, Redefining Development*. Geneva: UNISDR.

UNISDR (United Nations Office for Disaster Risk Reduction). 2015. *Global Assessment Report on Disaster Risk Reduction 2015: Making Development Sustainable: The Future of Disaster Risk Management*. Geneva: UNISDR.

Van Asseldonk, M. A., M. P. Meuwissen, and R. B. Huirne. 2002. 'Belief in Disaster Relief and the Demand for a Public–Private Insurance Program'. *Review of Agricultural Economics* 24: 196.

Van Wassenhove, L. N. 2006. 'Humanitarian Aid Logistics: Supply Chain Management in High Gear'. *Journal of the Operational Research Society* 57: 475.

Verdin, J., C. Funk, G. Senay, and R. Choularton. 2005. 'Climate Science and Famine Early Warning'. *Philosophical Transactions of the Royal Society* 360: 2155.

Von Peter, Goetz, Sebastian von Dahlen, and Sweta C. Saxena. 2012. 'Unmitigated Disasters? New Evidence on the Macroeconomic Cost of Natural Catastrophes'. BIS Working Paper No. 394, 1 December.

Von Ungern-Sternberg, T. 2004. *Efficient Monopolies: The Limits of Competition in the European Property Insurance Market*. Oxford: Oxford University Press.

WHO (World Health Organization). 2015. 'Report of the Ebola Interim Assessment Panel'. Geneva, July.

Wolde Mariam, Mesfin. 1986. 'Rural Vulnerability to Famine in Ethiopia: 1958–77'. London: Intermediate Technology Publications.

World Bank. 2010. *Natural Hazards, Unnatural Disasters: The Economics of Effective Prevention*. Washington: World Bank.

World Bank. 2012. 'FONDEN: Mexico's Natural Disaster Fund—A Review'. Washington <http://documents.worldbank.org/curated/en/2012/05/17291287/fonden-mexicos-natural-disaster-fund-review>.

World Bank. 2013. *Building Resilience: Integrating Climate and Disaster Risk into Development—Lessons from World Bank Group Experience*. Washington: World Bank.

World Bank. 2014a. *Financial Protection against Natural Disasters: An Operational Framework for Disaster Risk Financing and Insurance*. Washington: World Bank.

World Bank. 2014b. *World Development Report 2014: Risk and Opportunity: Managing Risk for Development*. Washington: World Bank.

World Bank. 2015. *Pacific Catastrophe Risk Insurance Pilot: From Design to Implementation: Some Lessons Learned*. Washington: World Bank.

Zeimpekis, Vasileios, Soumia Ichoua, and Ioannis Minis, eds. 2013. *Humanitarian and Relief Logistics*. London: Springer.

INDEX

Note: Page numbers in *italics* are for tables. Glossary page numbers are in **bold**.